WILLIAM SHAKESPEARE

ROMEO AND JULIET

CLASSICS

Published 2024

FiNGERPRINT! CLASSICS
Prakash Books

Fingerprint Publishing
@FingerprintP
@fingerprintpublishingbooks
www.fingerprintpublishing.com

ISBN: 978 93 8777 937 2

William Shakespeare began his career as an actor, writer, and part owner of a playing company called the Lord Chamberlain's Men, later known as King's Men, in London. Often regarded as the 'Bard of Avon' he is one of the world's pre-eminent dramatists. Born and brought up in Stratford-upon-Avon, he married Anne Hathaway at the age of eighteen and they had three children—Susanna, and twins Hamnet and Judith. Though few records survive of his private life, he appeared to have retired to Stratford around 1613 where he died three years later.

His works still in existence, including some collaborations, consist of thirty-eight plays, one hundred and fifty-four sonnets, two long narrative poems, and several other verses. His plays are performed much more than any other playwright's and have been translated in almost all major languages. Most of his known works have been produced between 1589 and 1613. His early plays were mainly comedies and histories which remain regarded as some of the best works produced in these genres.

Shakespeare's plays are difficult to date. His early classical and Italianate comedies contain tight double plots and precise comic sequences giving way to the romantic atmosphere of his most acclaimed comedies in the mid-1590s. *A Midsummer Night's Dream*—a witty mixture of romance, fairy magic, and comic low life scenes—is one of his most delightful creations shortly before he turned to *Romeo and Juliet*. *Romeo and Juliet* is his most famous romantic tragedy of sexually charged adolescence, love, and death. It marks a departure from his earlier works and from others of the English Renaissance.

His plays demonstrate the expansiveness of his imagination and the extent of his learning. Shakespeare's sequence of great comedies continue with *Merchant of Venice*, *Much Ado About Nothing*, *As You Like It*, and *Twelfth Night*. He introduced prose comedy in the histories of the late 1590s—*Henry IV, Part I* and *Henry V, Part II*—after the lyrical *Richard II*. *Julius Caesar* introduced a new kind of drama.

Shakespeare wrote the so-called 'problem plays' in the early 17th century. *Measure for Measure*, *Troilus and Cressida*, and *All's Well that Ends Well* being a few of them. Until about 1608, he mainly wrote tragedies including *Hamlet*, *Othello*, *King Lear*, and *Macbeth*. *Antony and Cleopatra* and *Coriolanus*—his last major tragedies, contain some of his finest poetry. Shakespeare wrote tragicomedies, also known as romances, in his last phase. These include *Cymbeline*, *The Winter's Tale*, and *The Tempest*, as well as the collaboration *Pericles, Prince of Tyre*.

A true genius, Shakespeare's popular characters and plots are studied, performed, reinterpreted, and discussed till today. William Shakespeare, known as the English national poet, is considered the greatest dramatist of all time.

THE CHARACTERS
IN THE PLAY

Escalus, PRINCE of Verona
MERCUTIO, kinsman of the Prince and friend
of Romeo PARIS, a young count, kinsman of the
Prince and Mercutio, and suitor of Juliet
PAGE to Count Paris
MONTAGUE, head of a Veronese family at feud
with the Capulets
LADY MONTAGUE
ROMEO, son of Montague
BENVOLIO, nephew of Montague and friend of
Romeo and Mercutio
ABRAM, servant of Montague
BALTHASAR, servant of Montague attending on
Romeo
CAPULET, head of a Veronese family at feud with
the Montagues

LADY CAPULET
JULIET, daughter of Capulet
TYBALT, nephew of Lady Capulet
FOLLOWER
COUSIN CAPULET, an old man of the Capulet family
NURSE of Juliet, her foster-mother
PETER, servant of Capulet attending on the Nurse
SAMPSON
GREGORY
CLOWN, a servant } of the Capulet household
SERVINGMEN
FRIAR LAURENCE, a Franciscan
FRIAR JOHN, a Franciscan
An APOTHECARY of Mantua
FIDDLER and MUSICIANS (Simon Catling, Hugh Rebeck, James Soundpost)
Members of the WATCH
CITIZENS of Verona
Maskers, torchbearers, pages, servants
CHORUS

THE MOST EXCELLENT AND LAMENTABLE TRAGEDY OF ROMEO AND JULIET

PROLOGUE

Two households, both alike in dignity,
In fair Verona, where we lay our scene,
From ancient grudge break to new mutiny,
Where civil blood makes civil hands unclean.
From forth the fatal loins of these two foes
A pair of star-cross'd lovers take their life;
Whose misadventured piteous overthrows
Do with their death bury their parents' strife.
The fearful passage of their death-mark'd love,
And the continuance of their parents' rage,
Which, but their children's end, nought
could remove,
Is now the two hours' traffic of our stage;
The which if you with patient ears attend,
What here shall miss, our toil shall strive to mend.

Act 1

SCENE I. VERONA. A PUBLIC PLACE.

Enter SAMPSON and GREGORY, of the house of Capulet, armed with swords and bucklers

SAMPSON
    Gregory, o' my word, we'll not carry coals.
GREGORY
    No, for then we should be colliers.
SAMPSON
    I mean, an we be in choler, we'll draw.
GREGORY
    Ay, while you live, draw your neck out o' the collar.
SAMPSON
    I strike quickly, being moved.

GREGORY

But thou art not quickly moved to strike.

SAMPSON

A dog of the house of Montague moves me.

GREGORY

To move is to stir; and to be valiant is to stand:
therefore, if thou art moved, thou runn'st away.

SAMPSON

A dog of that house shall move me to stand:
I will take the wall of any man or maid of
Montague's.

GREGORY

That shows thee a weak slave; for the weakest
goes to the wall.

SAMPSON

True; and therefore women, being the weaker
vessels, are ever thrust to the wall: therefore I
will push Montague's men from the wall, and
thrust his maids to the wall.

GREGORY

The quarrel is between our masters and us
their men.

SAMPSON

'Tis all one, I will show myself a tyrant: when I
have fought with the men, I will be cruel with
the maids, and cut off their heads.

GREGORY

The heads of the maids?

SAMPSON

Ay, the heads of the maids, or their maidenheads; take it in what sense thou wilt.

GREGORY

They must take it in sense that feel it.

SAMPSON

Me they shall feel while I am able to stand: and 'tis known I am a pretty piece of flesh.

GREGORY

'Tis well thou art not fish; if thou hadst, thou hadst been poor John. Draw thy tool! here comes two of the house of the Montagues.

SAMPSON

My naked weapon is out: quarrel, I will back thee.

GREGORY

How! turn thy back and run?

SAMPSON

Fear me not.

GREGORY

No, marry; I fear thee!

SAMPSON

Let us take the law of our sides; let them begin.

GREGORY

I will frown as I pass by, and let them take it
as they list.

SAMPSON

Nay, as they dare. I will bite my thumb at them;
which is a disgrace to them, if they bear it.

Enter ABRAHAM and BALTHASAR

ABRAHAM

Do you bite your thumb at us, sir?

SAMPSON

I do bite my thumb, sir.

ABRAHAM

Do you bite your thumb at us, sir?

SAMPSON

(Aside to GREGORY) Is the law of our side,
if I say ay?

GREGORY

No.

SAMPSON

No, sir, I do not bite my thumb at you, sir, but
I bite my thumb, sir.

GREGORY

Do you quarrel, sir?

ABRAHAM

Quarrel sir! no, sir.

SAMPSON

If you do, sir, I am for you: I serve as good a
man as you.

ABRAHAM

No better.

SAMPSON

Well, sir.

GREGORY

Say 'better:' here comes one of my master's
kinsmen.

SAMPSON

Yes, better, sir.

ABRAHAM

You lie.

SAMPSON

Draw, if you be men. Gregory, remember thy
swashing blow.

They fight
Enter BENVOLIO

BENVOLIO

Part, fools!
Put up your swords; you know not what you
do.
Beats down their swords

Enter TYBALT

TYBALT

What, art thou drawn among these heartless
hinds?

Turn thee, Benvolio, look upon thy death.

BENVOLIO

I do but keep the peace: put up thy sword,

Or manage it to part these men with me.

TYBALT

What, drawn, and talk of peace! I hate the
word,

As I hate hell, all Montagues, and thee:

Have at thee, coward!

They fight

*Enter, several of both houses, who join the fray; then enter
Citizens, with clubs*

FIRST CITIZEN

Clubs, bills, and partisans! strike! beat them
down!

Down with the Capulets! down with the
Montagues!

Enter CAPULET *in his gown, and* LADY CAPULET

CAPULET

What noise is this? Give me my long sword,
ho!

LADY CAPULET

A crutch, a crutch! why call you for a sword?

CAPULET

My sword, I say! Old Montague is come,
And flourishes his blade in spite of me.

Enter MONTAGUE and LADY MONTAGUE

MONTAGUE

Thou villain Capulet,—Hold me not, let me
go.

LADY MONTAGUE

Thou shalt not stir a foot to seek a foe.

Enter PRINCE, with Attendants

PRINCE

Rebellious subjects, enemies to peace,
Profaners of this neighbour-stained steel,—
Will they not hear? What, ho! you men, you
beasts,
That quench the fire of your pernicious rage
With purple fountains issuing from your veins,
On pain of torture, from those bloody hands
Throw your mistemper'd weapons to the
ground,
And hear the sentence of your moved prince.
Three civil brawls, bred of an airy word,
By thee, old Capulet, and Montague,

Have thrice disturb'd the quiet of our streets,
And made Verona's ancient citizens
Cast by their grave beseeming ornaments,
To wield old partisans, in hands as old,
Canker'd with peace, to part your canker'd
 hate:
If ever you disturb our streets again,
Your lives shall pay the forfeit of the peace.
For this time, all the rest depart away:
You Capulet; shall go along with me:
And, Montague, come you this afternoon,
To know our further pleasure in this case,
To old Free-town, our common judgment-
 place.
Once more, on pain of death, all men depart.

    Exeunt all but MONTAGUE, LADY
     MONTAGUE, *and* BENVOLIO

MONTAGUE

Who set this ancient quarrel new abroach?
Speak, nephew, were you by when it began?

BENVOLIO

Here were the servants of your adversary,
And yours, close fighting ere I did approach:
I drew to part them: in the instant came
The fiery Tybalt, with his sword prepared,
Which, as he breathed defiance to my ears,
He swung about his head and cut the winds,

Who nothing hurt withal hiss'd him in scorn:
While we were interchanging thrusts and blows,
Came more and more and fought on part and
    part,
Till the prince came, who parted either part.

LADY MONTAGUE

O, where is Romeo? saw you him to-day?
Right glad I am he was not at this fray.

BENVOLIO

Madam, an hour before the worshipp'd sun
Peer'd forth the golden window of the east,
A troubled mind drave me to walk abroad;
Where, underneath the grove of sycamore
That westward rooteth from the city's side,
So early walking did I see your son:
Towards him I made, but he was ware of me
And stole into the covert of the wood:
I, measuring his affections by my own,
That most are busied when they're most alone,
Pursued my humour not pursuing his,
And gladly shunn'd who gladly fled from me.

MONTAGUE

Many a morning hath he there been seen,
With tears augmenting the fresh morning dew.
Adding to clouds more clouds with his deep
    sighs;
But all so soon as the all-cheering sun

Should in the furthest east begin to draw
The shady curtains from Aurora's bed,
Away from the light steals home my heavy son,
And private in his chamber pens himself,
Shuts up his windows, locks far daylight out
And makes himself an artificial night:
Black and portentous must this humour prove,
Unless good counsel may the cause remove.

BENVOLIO

My noble uncle, do you know the cause?

MONTAGUE

I neither know it nor can learn of him.

BENVOLIO

Have you importuned him by any means?

MONTAGUE

Both by myself and many other friends:
But he, his own affections' counsellor,
Is to himself—I will not say how true—
But to himself so secret and so close,
So far from sounding and discovery,
As is the bud bit with an envious worm,
Ere he can spread his sweet leaves to the air,
Or dedicate his beauty to the sun.
Could we but learn from whence his sorrows
        grow.
We would as willingly give cure as know.

Enter ROMEO

BENVOLIO

    See, where he comes: so please you, step aside;

    I'll know his grievance, or be much denied.

MONTAGUE

    I would thou wert so happy by thy stay,

    To hear true shrift. Come, madam, let's away.

Exeunt MONTAGUE and LADY MONTAGUE

BENVOLIO

    Good-morrow, cousin.

ROMEO

    Is the day so young?

BENVOLIO

    But new struck nine.

ROMEO

    Ay me! sad hours seem long.

    Was that my father that went hence so fast?

BENVOLIO

    It was. What sadness lengthens Romeo's hours?

ROMEO

    Not having that, which, having, makes them short.

BENVOLIO

    In love?

ROMEO

    Out—

BENVOLIO

Of love?

ROMEO

Out of her favour, where I am in love.

BENVOLIO

Alas, that love, so gentle in his view,

Should be so tyrannous and rough in proof!

ROMEO

Alas, that love, whose view is muffled still,

Should, without eyes, see pathways to his will!

Where shall we dine? O me! What fray was here?

Yet tell me not, for I have heard it all.

Here's much to do with hate, but more with
     love.

Why, then, O brawling love! O loving hate!

O any thing, of nothing first create!

O heavy lightness! serious vanity!

Mis-shapen chaos of well-seeming forms!

Feather of lead, bright smoke, cold fire, sick
     health!

Still-waking sleep, that is not what it is!

This love feel I, that feel no love in this.

Dost thou not laugh?

BENVOLIO

No, coz, I rather weep.

ROMEO

Good heart, at what?

BENVOLIO

At thy good heart's oppression.

ROMEO

Why, such is love's transgression.
Griefs of mine own lie heavy in my breast,
Which thou wilt propagate, to have it prest
With more of thine: this love that thou hast
shown
Doth add more grief to too much of mine
own.
Love is a smoke raised with the fume of sighs;
Being purged, a fire sparkling in lovers' eyes;
Being vex'd a sea nourish'd with lovers' tears:
What is it else? a madness most discreet,
A choking gall and a preserving sweet.
Farewell, my coz.

BENVOLIO

Soft! I will go along;
An if you leave me so, you do me wrong.

ROMEO

Tut, I have lost myself; I am not here;
This is not Romeo, he's some other where.

BENVOLIO

Tell me in sadness, who is that you love.

ROMEO

What, shall I groan and tell thee?

BENVOLIO

Groan! why, no.

But sadly tell me who.

ROMEO

Bid a sick man in sadness make his will:

Ah, word ill urged to one that is so ill!

In sadness, cousin, I do love a woman.

BENVOLIO

I aim'd so near, when I supposed you loved.

ROMEO

A right good mark-man! And she's fair I love.

BENVOLIO

A right fair mark, fair coz, is soonest hit.

ROMEO

Well, in that hit you miss: she'll not be hit

With Cupid's arrow; she hath Dian's wit;

And, in strong proof of chastity well arm'd,

From love's weak childish bow she lives
    unharm'd.

She will not stay the siege of loving terms,

Nor bide the encounter of assailing eyes,

Nor ope her lap to saint-seducing gold:

O, she is rich in beauty, only poor,

That when she dies with beauty dies her store.

BENVOLIO

Then she hath sworn that she will still live chaste?

ROMEO

> She hath, and in that sparing makes huge
> > waste,
>
> For beauty starved with her severity
> Cuts beauty off from all posterity.
> She is too fair, too wise, wisely too fair,
> To merit bliss by making me despair:
> She hath forsworn to love, and in that vow
> Do I live dead that live to tell it now.

BENVOLIO

> Be ruled by me, forget to think of her.

ROMEO

> O, teach me how I should forget to think.

BENVOLIO

> By giving liberty unto thine eyes;
> Examine other beauties.

ROMEO

> 'Tis the way
> To call hers exquisite, in question more:
> These happy masks that kiss fair ladies' brows
> Being black put us in mind they hide the fair;
> He that is strucken blind cannot forget
> The precious treasure of his eyesight lost:
> Show me a mistress that is passing fair,
> What doth her beauty serve, but as a note
> Where I may read who pass'd that passing fair?
> Farewell: thou canst not teach me to forget.

BENVOLIO

I'll pay that doctrine, or else die in debt.

Exeunt

SCENE II. A STREET.

Enter CAPULET, PARIS, and Servant

CAPULET

But Montague is bound as well as I,
In penalty alike; and 'tis not hard, I think,
For men so old as we to keep the peace.

PARIS

Of honourable reckoning are you both;
And pity 'tis you lived at odds so long.
But now, my lord, what say you to my suit?

CAPULET

But saying o'er what I have said before:
My child is yet a stranger in the world;
She hath not seen the change of fourteen
     years,
Let two more summers wither in their pride,
Ere we may think her ripe to be a bride.

PARIS

Younger than she are happy mothers made.

CAPULET

And too soon marr'd are those so early made.
The earth hath swallow'd all my hopes but she,

She is the hopeful lady of my earth:
But woo her, gentle Paris, get her heart,
My will to her consent is but a part;
An she agree, within her scope of choice
Lies my consent and fair according voice.
This night I hold an old accustom'd feast,
Whereto I have invited many a guest,
Such as I love; and you, among the store,
One more, most welcome, makes my number
     more.
At my poor house look to behold this night
Earth-treading stars that make dark heaven
     light:
Such comfort as do lusty young men feel
When well-apparell'd April on the heel
Of limping winter treads, even such delight
Among fresh female buds shall you this night
Inherit at my house; hear all, all see,
And like her most whose merit most shall be:
Which on more view, of many mine being
     one
May stand in number, though in reckoning
     none,
Come, go with me.
To Servant, giving a paper
Go, sirrah, trudge about
Through fair Verona; find those persons out

29

Whose names are written there, and to them say,
My house and welcome on their pleasure stay.

Exeunt CAPULET and PARIS

SERVANT

Find them out whose names are written here!
It is written, that the shoemaker should meddle
with his yard, and the tailor with his last, the
fisher with his pencil, and the painter with his
nets; but I am sent to find those persons whose
names are here writ, and can never find what
names the writing person hath here writ. I
must to the learned.—In good time.

Enter BENVOLIO and ROMEO

BENVOLIO

Tut, man, one fire burns out another's burning,
One pain is lessen'd by another's anguish;
Turn giddy, and be holp by backward turning;
One desperate grief cures with another's
    languish:
Take thou some new infection to thy eye,
And the rank poison of the old will die.

ROMEO

Your plaintain-leaf is excellent for that.

BENVOLIO

For what, I pray thee?

ROMEO

For your broken shin.

BENVOLIO

Why, Romeo, art thou mad?

ROMEO

Not mad, but bound more than a mad-man is;
Shut up in prison, kept without my food,
Whipp'd and tormented and—God-den, good
    fellow.

SERVANT

God gi' god-den. I pray, sir, can you read?

ROMEO

Ay, mine own fortune in my misery.

SERVANT

Perhaps you have learned it without book: but,
I pray, can you read any thing you see?

ROMEO

Ay, if I know the letters and the language.

SERVANT

Ye say honestly: rest you merry!

ROMEO

Stay, fellow; I can read.
Reads
'Signior Martino and his wife and daughters;
County Anselme and his beauteous sisters;
the lady widow of Vitravio; Signior Placentio

and his lovely nieces; Mercutio and his brother
Valentine; mine uncle Capulet, his wife and
daughters; my fair niece Rosaline; Livia;
Signior Valentio and his cousin Tybalt, Lucio
and the lively Helena.' A fair assembly: whither
should they come?

SERVANT

Up.

ROMEO

Whither?

SERVANT

To supper; to our house.

ROMEO

Whose house?

SERVANT

My master's.

ROMEO

Indeed, I should have ask'd you that before.

SERVANT

Now I'll tell you without asking: my master is
the great rich Capulet; and if you be not of the
house of Montagues, I pray, come and crush a
cup of wine. Rest you merry!

Exit

BENVOLIO

At this same ancient feast of Capulet's
Sups the fair Rosaline whom thou so lovest,

With all the admired beauties of Verona:
Go thither; and, with unattainted eye,
Compare her face with some that I shall show,
And I will make thee think thy swan a crow.

ROMEO

When the devout religion of mine eye
Maintains such falsehood, then turn tears to
    fires;
And these, who often drown'd could never die,
Transparent heretics, be burnt for liars!
One fairer than my love! the all-seeing sun
Ne'er saw her match since first the world begun.

BENVOLIO

Tut, you saw her fair, none else being by,
Herself poised with herself in either eye:
But in that crystal scales let there be weigh'd
Your lady's love against some other maid
That I will show you shining at this feast,
And she shall scant show well that now shows
    best.

ROMEO

I'll go along, no such sight to be shown,
But to rejoice in splendor of mine own.

Exeunt

SCENE III. A ROOM IN CAPULET'S HOUSE.

Enter LADY CAPULET and NURSE

LADY CAPULET

    Nurse, where's my daughter? call her forth to
    me.

NURSE

    Now, by my maidenhead, at twelve year old,
    I bade her come. What, lamb! what, ladybird!
    God forbid! Where's this girl? What, Juliet!

Enter JULIET

JULIET

    How now! who calls?

NURSE

    Your mother.

JULIET

    Madam, I am here.
    What is your will?

LADY CAPULET

    This is the matter:—Nurse, give leave awhile,
    We must talk in secret:—nurse, come back again;
    I have remember'd me, thou's hear our counsel.
    Thou know'st my daughter's of a pretty age.

NURSE

    Faith, I can tell her age unto an hour.

LADY CAPULET

    She's not fourteen.

NURSE

    I'll lay fourteen of my teeth,—

    And yet, to my teeth be it spoken, I have but

        four—

    She is not fourteen. How long is it now

    To Lammas-tide?

LADY CAPULET

    A fortnight and odd days.

NURSE

    Even or odd, of all days in the year,

    Come Lammas-eve at night shall she be

        fourteen.

    Susan and she—God rest all Christian souls!—

    Were of an age: well, Susan is with God;

    She was too good for me: but, as I said,

    On Lammas-eve at night shall she be fourteen;

    That shall she, marry; I remember it well.

    'Tis since the earthquake now eleven years;

    And she was wean'd,—I never shall forget

        it,—

    Of all the days of the year, upon that day:

    For I had then laid wormwood to my dug,

    Sitting in the sun under the dove-house wall;

    My lord and you were then at Mantua:—

    Nay, I do bear a brain:—but, as I said,

When it did taste the wormwood on the nipple
Of my dug and felt it bitter, pretty fool,
To see it tetchy and fall out with the dug!
Shake quoth the dove-house: 'twas no need, I
    trow,
To bid me trudge:
And since that time it is eleven years;
For then she could stand alone; nay, by the rood,
She could have run and waddled all about;
For even the day before, she broke her brow:
And then my husband—God be with his soul!
A' was a merry man—took up the child:
'Yea,' quoth he, 'dost thou fall upon thy face?
Thou wilt fall backward when thou hast more
    wit;
Wilt thou not, Jule?' and, by my holidame,
The pretty wretch left crying and said 'Ay.'
To see, now, how a jest shall come about!
I warrant, an I should live a thousand years,
I never should forget it: 'Wilt thou not, Jule?'
    quoth he;
And, pretty fool, it stinted and said 'Ay.'
LADY CAPULET
Enough of this; I pray thee, hold thy peace.
NURSE
Yes, madam: yet I cannot choose but laugh,
To think it should leave crying and say 'Ay.'

And yet, I warrant, it had upon its brow
A bump as big as a young cockerel's stone;
A parlous knock; and it cried bitterly:
'Yea,' quoth my husband, 'fall'st upon thy face?
Thou wilt fall backward when thou comest to
     age;
Wilt thou not, Jule?' it stinted and said 'Ay.'

JULIET

And stint thou too, I pray thee, nurse, say I.

NURSE

Peace, I have done. God mark thee to his grace!
Thou wast the prettiest babe that e'er I nursed:
An I might live to see thee married once,
I have my wish.

LADY CAPULET

Marry, that 'marry' is the very theme
I came to talk of. Tell me, daughter Juliet,
How stands your disposition to be married?

JULIET

It is an honour that I dream not of.

NURSE

An honour! were not I thine only nurse,
I would say thou hadst suck'd wisdom from
     thy teat.

LADY CAPULET

Well, think of marriage now; younger than you,
Here in Verona, ladies of esteem,

Are made already mothers: by my count,
I was your mother much upon these years
That you are now a maid. Thus then in brief:
The valiant Paris seeks you for his love.

NURSE

A man, young lady! lady, such a man
As all the world—why, he's a man of wax.

LADY CAPULET

Verona's summer hath not such a flower.

NURSE

Nay, he's a flower; in faith, a very flower.

LADY CAPULET

What say you? can you love the gentleman?
This night you shall behold him at our feast;
Read o'er the volume of young Paris' face,
And find delight writ there with beauty's pen;
Examine every married lineament,
And see how one another lends content
And what obscured in this fair volume lies
Find written in the margent of his eyes.
This precious book of love, this unbound
        lover,
To beautify him, only lacks a cover:
The fish lives in the sea, and 'tis much pride
For fair without the fair within to hide:
That book in many's eyes doth share the glory,
That in gold clasps locks in the golden story;

So shall you share all that he doth possess,
By having him, making yourself no less.
NURSE
No less! nay, bigger; women grow by men.
LADY CAPULET
Speak briefly, can you like of Paris' love?
JULIET
I'll look to like, if looking liking move:
But no more deep will I endart mine eye
Than your consent gives strength to make it fly.

Enter a Servant
SERVANT
Madam, the guests are come, supper served
up, you called, my young lady asked for, the
nurse cursed in the pantry, and every thing in
extremity. I must hence to wait; I beseech you,
follow straight.
LADY CAPULET
We follow thee.

Exit Servant

Juliet, the county stays.
NURSE
Go, girl, seek happy nights to happy days.

Exeunt

SCENE IV. A STREET.

Enter ROMEO, MERCUTIO, BENVOLIO, with five or six Maskers, Torch-bearers, and others

ROMEO

What, shall this speech be spoke for our
    excuse?
Or shall we on without a apology?

BENVOLIO

The date is out of such prolixity:
We'll have no Cupid hoodwink'd with a scarf,
Bearing a Tartar's painted bow of lath,
Scaring the ladies like a crow-keeper;
Nor no without-book prologue, faintly spoke
After the prompter, for our entrance:
But let them measure us by what they will;
We'll measure them a measure, and be gone.

ROMEO

Give me a torch: I am not for this ambling;
Being but heavy, I will bear the light.

MERCUTIO

Nay, gentle Romeo, we must have you dance.

ROMEO

Not I, believe me: you have dancing shoes
With nimble soles: I have a soul of lead
So stakes me to the ground I cannot move.

MERCUTIO

You are a lover; borrow Cupid's wings,
And soar with them above a common bound.

ROMEO

I am too sore enpierced with his shaft
To soar with his light feathers, and so bound,
I cannot bound a pitch above dull woe:
Under love's heavy burden do I sink.

MERCUTIO

And, to sink in it, should you burden love;
Too great oppression for a tender thing.

ROMEO

Is love a tender thing? it is too rough,
Too rude, too boisterous, and it pricks like
thorn.

MERCUTIO

If love be rough with you, be rough with love;
Prick love for pricking, and you beat love
down.
Give me a case to put my visage in:
A visor for a visor! what care I
What curious eye doth quote deformities?
Here are the beetle brows shall blush for me.

BENVOLIO

Come, knock and enter; and no sooner in,
But every man betake him to his legs.

ROMEO

A torch for me: let wantons light of heart
Tickle the senseless rushes with their heels,
For I am proverb'd with a grandsire phrase;
I'll be a candle-holder, and look on.
The game was ne'er so fair, and I am done.

MERCUTIO

Tut, dun's the mouse, the constable's own word:
If thou art dun, we'll draw thee from the mire
Of this sir-reverence love, wherein thou stick'st
Up to the ears. Come, we burn daylight, ho!

ROMEO

Nay, that's not so.

MERCUTIO

I mean, sir, in delay
We waste our lights in vain, like lamps by day.
Take our good meaning, for our judgment sits
Five times in that ere once in our five wits.

ROMEO

And we mean well in going to this mask;
But 'tis no wit to go.

MERCUTIO

Why, may one ask?

ROMEO

I dream'd a dream to-night.

MERCUTIO

And so did I.

ROMEO
    Well, what was yours?
MERCUTIO
    That dreamers often lie.
ROMEO
    In bed asleep, while they do dream things true.
MERCUTIO
    O, then, I see Queen Mab hath been with you.
    She is the fairies' midwife, and she comes
    In shape no bigger than an agate-stone
    On the fore-finger of an alderman,
    Drawn with a team of little atomies
    Athwart men's noses as they lie asleep;
    Her wagon-spokes made of long spiders' legs,
    The cover of the wings of grasshoppers,
    The traces of the smallest spider's web,
    The collars of the moonshine's watery beams,
    Her whip of cricket's bone, the lash of film,
    Her wagoner a small grey-coated gnat,
    Not so big as a round little worm
    Prick'd from the lazy finger of a maid;
    Her chariot is an empty hazel-nut
    Made by the joiner squirrel or old grub,
    Time out o' mind the fairies' coachmakers.
    And in this state she gallops night by night
    Through lovers' brains, and then they dream
        of love;

O'er courtiers' knees, that dream on court'sies
    straight,
O'er lawyers' fingers, who straight dream on
    fees,
O'er ladies' lips, who straight on kisses dream,
Which oft the angry Mab with blisters plagues,
Because their breaths with sweetmeats tainted
    are:
Sometime she gallops o'er a courtier's nose,
And then dreams he of smelling out a suit;
And sometime comes she with a tithe-pig's tail
Tickling a parson's nose as a' lies asleep,
Then dreams, he of another benefice:
Sometime she driveth o'er a soldier's neck,
And then dreams he of cutting foreign throats,
Of breaches, ambuscadoes, Spanish blades,
Of healths five-fathom deep; and then anon
Drums in his ear, at which he starts and wakes,
And being thus frighted swears a prayer or two
And sleeps again. This is that very Mab
That plats the manes of horses in the night,
And bakes the elflocks in foul sluttish hairs,
Which once untangled, much misfortune bodes:
This is the hag, when maids lie on their backs,
That presses them and learns them first to bear,
Making them women of good carriage:
This is she—

ROMEO

Peace, peace, Mercutio, peace!
Thou talk'st of nothing.

MERCUTIO

True, I talk of dreams,
Which are the children of an idle brain,
Begot of nothing but vain fantasy,
Which is as thin of substance as the air
And more inconstant than the wind, who wooes
Even now the frozen bosom of the north,
And, being anger'd, puffs away from thence,
Turning his face to the dew-dropping south.

BENVOLIO

This wind, you talk of, blows us from ourselves;
Supper is done, and we shall come too late.

ROMEO

I fear, too early: for my mind misgives
Some consequence yet hanging in the stars
Shall bitterly begin his fearful date
With this night's revels and expire the term
Of a despised life closed in my breast
By some vile forfeit of untimely death.
But He, that hath the steerage of my course,
Direct my sail! On, lusty gentlemen.

BENVOLIO

Strike, drum.

Exeunt

SCENE V. A HALL IN CAPULET'S HOUSE.

Musicians waiting. Enter Servingmen with napkins

FIRST SERVANT

Where's Potpan, that he helps not to take away? He shift a trencher? he scrape a trencher!

SECOND SERVANT

When good manners shall lie all in one or two men's hands and they unwashed too, 'tis a foul thing.

FIRST SERVANT

Away with the joint-stools, remove the court-cupboard, look to the plate. Good thou, save me a piece of marchpane; and, as thou lovest me, let the porter let in Susan Grindstone and Nell. Antony, and Potpan!

SECOND SERVANT

Ay, boy, ready.

FIRST SERVANT

You are looked for and called for, asked for and sought for, in the great chamber.

SECOND SERVANT

We cannot be here and there too. Cheerly, boys; be brisk awhile, and the longer liver take all.

Enter CAPULET, with JULIET and others of his house,
meeting the Guests and Maskers

CAPULET

Welcome, gentlemen! ladies that have their toes
Unplagued with corns will have a bout with
you.
Ah ha, my mistresses! which of you all
Will now deny to dance? she that makes dainty,
She, I'll swear, hath corns; am I come near ye
now?
Welcome, gentlemen! I have seen the day
That I have worn a visor and could tell
A whispering tale in a fair lady's ear,
Such as would please: 'tis gone, 'tis gone, 'tis
gone:
You are welcome, gentlemen! come, musicians,
play.
A hall, a hall! give room! and foot it, girls.
Music plays, and they dance
More light, you knaves; and turn the tables up,
And quench the fire, the room is grown too hot.
Ah, sirrah, this unlook'd-for sport comes well.
Nay, sit, nay, sit, good cousin Capulet;
For you and I are past our dancing days:
How long is't now since last yourself and I
Were in a mask?

SECOND CAPULET

By'r lady, thirty years.

CAPULET

What, man! 'tis not so much, 'tis not so much:

'Tis since the nuptials of Lucentio,

Come pentecost as quickly as it will,

Some five and twenty years; and then we mask'd.

SECOND CAPULET

'Tis more, 'tis more, his son is elder, sir;

His son is thirty.

CAPULET

Will you tell me that?

His son was but a ward two years ago.

ROMEO

(To a Servingman) What lady is that, which

doth enrich the hand of yonder knight?

SERVANT

I know not, sir.

ROMEO

O, she doth teach the torches to burn bright!

It seems she hangs upon the cheek of night

Like a rich jewel in an Ethiope's ear;

Beauty too rich for use, for earth too dear!

So shows a snowy dove trooping with crows,

As yonder lady o'er her fellows shows.

The measure done, I'll watch her place of stand,

And, touching hers, make blessed my rude hand.

Did my heart love till now? forswear it, sight!
For I ne'er saw true beauty till this night.

TYBALT

This, by his voice, should be a Montague.
Fetch me my rapier, boy. What dares the slave
Come hither, cover'd with an antic face,
To fleer and scorn at our solemnity?
Now, by the stock and honour of my kin,
To strike him dead, I hold it not a sin.

CAPULET

Why, how now, kinsman! wherefore storm you
so?

TYBALT

Uncle, this is a Montague, our foe,
A villain that is hither come in spite,
To scorn at our solemnity this night.

CAPULET

Young Romeo is it?

TYBALT

'Tis he, that villain Romeo.

CAPULET

Content thee, gentle coz, let him alone;
He bears him like a portly gentleman;
And, to say truth, Verona brags of him
To be a virtuous and well-govern'd youth:
I would not for the wealth of all the town
Here in my house do him disparagement:

Therefore be patient, take no note of him:
It is my will, the which if thou respect,
Show a fair presence and put off these frowns,
And ill-beseeming semblance for a feast.

TYBALT

It fits, when such a villain is a guest:
I'll not endure him.

CAPULET

He shall be endured:
What, goodman boy! I say, he shall: go to;
Am I the master here, or you? go to.
You'll not endure him! God shall mend my
soul!
You'll make a mutiny among my guests!
You will set cock-a-hoop! you'll be the man!

TYBALT

Why, uncle, 'tis a shame.

CAPULET

Go to, go to;
You are a saucy boy: is't so, indeed?
This trick may chance to scathe you, I know
what:
You must contrary me! marry, 'tis time.
Well said, my hearts! You are a princox; go:
Be quiet, or—More light, more light! For
shame!
I'll make you quiet. What, cheerly, my hearts!

TYBALT

> Patience perforce with wilful choler meeting
> Makes my flesh tremble in their different
>> greeting.
> I will withdraw: but this intrusion shall
> Now seeming sweet convert to bitter gall.

> *Exit*

ROMEO

> (To JULIET) If I profane with my unworthiest
>> hand
> This holy shrine, the gentle fine is this:
> My lips, two blushing pilgrims, ready stand
> To smooth that rough touch with a tender kiss.

JULIET

> Good pilgrim, you do wrong your hand too
>> much,
> Which mannerly devotion shows in this;
> For saints have hands that pilgrims' hands do
>> touch,
> And palm to palm is holy palmers' kiss.

ROMEO

> Have not saints lips, and holy palmers too?

JULIET

> Ay, pilgrim, lips that they must use in prayer.

ROMEO

> O, then, dear saint, let lips do what hands do;
> They pray, grant thou, lest faith turn to despair.

JULIET

Saints do not move, though grant for prayers'
    sake.

ROMEO

Then move not, while my prayer's effect I take.

Thus from my lips, by yours, my sin is purged.

JULIET

Then have my lips the sin that they have took.

ROMEO

Sin from thy lips? O trespass sweetly urged!

Give me my sin again.

JULIET

You kiss by the book.

NURSE

Madam, your mother craves a word with you.

ROMEO

What is her mother?

NURSE

Marry, bachelor,

Her mother is the lady of the house,

And a good lady, and a wise and virtuous

I nursed her daughter, that you talk'd withal;

I tell you, he that can lay hold of her

Shall have the chinks.

ROMEO

Is she a Capulet?

O dear account! my life is my foe's debt.

BENVOLIO

Away, begone; the sport is at the best.

ROMEO

Ay, so I fear; the more is my unrest.

CAPULET

Nay, gentlemen, prepare not to be gone;
We have a trifling foolish banquet towards.
Is it e'en so? why, then, I thank you all
I thank you, honest gentlemen; good night.
More torches here! Come on then, let's to bed.
Ah, sirrah, by my fay, it waxes late:
I'll to my rest.

*Exeunt all but JULIET
and Nurse*

JULIET

Come hither, nurse. What is yond gentleman?

NURSE

The son and heir of old Tiberio.

JULIET

What's he that now is going out of door?

NURSE

Marry, that, I think, be young Petrucio.

JULIET

What's he that follows there, that would not
dance?

NURSE

I know not.

JULIET

Go ask his name: if he be married.

My grave is like to be my wedding bed.

NURSE

His name is Romeo, and a Montague;

The only son of your great enemy.

JULIET

My only love sprung from my only hate!

Too early seen unknown, and known too late!

Prodigious birth of love it is to me,

That I must love a loathed enemy.

NURSE

What's this? what's this?

JULIET

A rhyme I learn'd even now

Of one I danced withal.

One calls within 'Juliet.'

NURSE

Anon, anon!

Come, let's away; the strangers all are gone.

Exeunt

Act 2

Enter Chorus

CHORUS

Now old desire doth in his death-bed lie,
And young affection gapes to be his heir;
That fair for which love groan'd for and would
    die,
With tender Juliet match'd, is now not fair.
Now Romeo is beloved and loves again,
Alike betwitched by the charm of looks,
But to his foe supposed he must complain,
And she steal love's sweet bait from fearful
    hooks:
Being held a foe, he may not have access
To breathe such vows as lovers use to swear;
And she as much in love, her means much less
To meet her new-beloved any where:

But passion lends them power, time means, to
    meet
Tempering extremities with extreme sweet.

Exit

SCENE I. A LANE BY THE WALL
OF CAPULET'S ORCHARD.

Enter ROMEO
ROMEO

Can I go forward when my heart is here?
Turn back, dull earth, and find thy centre out.
He climbs the wall, and leaps down within it

Enter BENVOLIO and MERCUTIO
BENVOLIO

Romeo! my cousin Romeo!
MERCUTIO

He is wise;
And, on my lie, hath stol'n him home to bed.
BENVOLIO

He ran this way, and leap'd this orchard wall:
Call, good Mercutio.
MERCUTIO

Nay, I'll conjure too.
Romeo! humours! madman! passion! lover!
Appear thou in the likeness of a sigh:

Speak but one rhyme, and I am satisfied;
Cry but 'Ay me!' pronounce but 'love' and
    'dove;'
Speak to my gossip Venus one fair word,
One nick-name for her purblind son and heir,
Young Adam Cupid, he that shot so trim,
When King Cophetua loved the beggar-maid!
He heareth not, he stirreth not, he moveth not;
The ape is dead, and I must conjure him.
I conjure thee by Rosaline's bright eyes,
By her high forehead and her scarlet lip,
By her fine foot, straight leg and quivering
    thigh
And the demesnes that there adjacent lie,
That in thy likeness thou appear to us!

BENVOLIO

And if he hear thee, thou wilt anger him.

MERCUTIO

This cannot anger him: 'twould anger him
To raise a spirit in his mistress' circle
Of some strange nature, letting it there stand
Till she had laid it and conjured it down;
That were some spite: my invocation
Is fair and honest, and in his mistress' name
I conjure only but to raise up him.

BENVOLIO

Come, he hath hid himself among these trees,

To be consorted with the humorous night:
Blind is his love and best befits the dark.

MERCUTIO

If love be blind, love cannot hit the mark.
Now will he sit under a medlar tree,
And wish his mistress were that kind of fruit
As maids call medlars, when they laugh alone.
Romeo, that she were, O, that she were
An open et caetera, thou a poperin pear!
Romeo, good night: I'll to my truckle-bed;
This field-bed is too cold for me to sleep:
Come, shall we go?

BENVOLIO

Go, then; for 'tis in vain
To seek him here that means not to be found.

Exeunt

SCENE II. CAPULET'S ORCHARD.

Enter ROMEO
ROMEO
    He jests at scars that never felt a wound.
    JULIET appears above at a window
    But, soft! what light through yonder window
        breaks?
    It is the east, and Juliet is the sun.
    Arise, fair sun, and kill the envious moon,
    Who is already sick and pale with grief,
    That thou her maid art far more fair than she:
    Be not her maid, since she is envious;
    Her vestal livery is but sick and green
    And none but fools do wear it; cast it off.
    It is my lady, O, it is my love!
    O, that she knew she were!
    She speaks yet she says nothing: what of that?
    Her eye discourses; I will answer it.
    I am too bold, 'tis not to me she speaks:
    Two of the fairest stars in all the heaven,
    Having some business, do entreat her eyes
    To twinkle in their spheres till they return.
    What if her eyes were there, they in her head?
    The brightness of her cheek would shame
        those stars,
    As daylight doth a lamp; her eyes in heaven

Would through the airy region stream so
   bright
That birds would sing and think it were not
   night.
See, how she leans her cheek upon her hand!
O, that I were a glove upon that hand,
That I might touch that cheek!

JULIET

Ay me!

ROMEO

She speaks:
O, speak again, bright angel! for thou art
As glorious to this night, being o'er my head
As is a winged messenger of heaven
Unto the white-upturned wondering eyes
Of mortals that fall back to gaze on him
When he bestrides the lazy-pacing clouds
And sails upon the bosom of the air.

JULIET

O Romeo, Romeo! wherefore art thou
   Romeo?
Deny thy father and refuse thy name;
Or, if thou wilt not, be but sworn my love,
And I'll no longer be a Capulet.

ROMEO

(Aside) Shall I hear more, or shall I speak at
this?

JULIET

’Tis but thy name that is my enemy;
Thou art thyself, though not a Montague.
What’s Montague? it is nor hand, nor foot,
Nor arm, nor face, nor any other part
Belonging to a man. O, be some other name!
What’s in a name? that which we call a rose
By any other name would smell as sweet;
So Romeo would, were he not Romeo call’d,
Retain that dear perfection which he owes
Without that title. Romeo, doff thy name,
And for that name which is no part of thee
Take all myself.

ROMEO

I take thee at thy word:
Call me but love, and I’ll be new baptized;
Henceforth I never will be Romeo.

JULIET

What man art thou that thus bescreen’d in
night So stumblest on my counsel?

ROMEO

By a name
I know not how to tell thee who I am:
My name, dear saint, is hateful to myself,
Because it is an enemy to thee;
Had I it written, I would tear the word.

JULIET

My ears have not yet drunk a hundred words
Of that tongue's utterance, yet I know the sound:
Art thou not Romeo and a Montague?

ROMEO

Neither, fair saint, if either thee dislike.

JULIET

How camest thou hither, tell me, and
    wherefore?
The orchard walls are high and hard to climb,
And the place death, considering who thou art,
If any of my kinsmen find thee here.

ROMEO

With love's light wings did I o'er-perch these
    walls;
For stony limits cannot hold love out,
And what love can do that dares love attempt;
Therefore thy kinsmen are no let to me.

JULIET

If they do see thee, they will murder thee.

ROMEO

Alack, there lies more peril in thine eye
Than twenty of their swords: look thou but
    sweet,
And I am proof against their enmity.

JULIET

I would not for the world they saw thee here.

ROMEO

    I have night's cloak to hide me from their sight;

    And but thou love me, let them find me here:

    My life were better ended by their hate,

    Than death prorogued, wanting of thy love.

JULIET

    By whose direction found'st thou out this place?

ROMEO

    By love, who first did prompt me to inquire;

    He lent me counsel and I lent him eyes.

    I am no pilot; yet, wert thou as far

    As that vast shore wash'd with the farthest sea,

    I would adventure for such merchandise.

JULIET

    Thou know'st the mask of night is on my face,

    Else would a maiden blush bepaint my cheek

    For that which thou hast heard me speak to-

        night

    Fain would I dwell on form, fain, fain deny

    What I have spoke: but farewell compliment!

    Dost thou love me? I know thou wilt say 'Ay,'

    And I will take thy word: yet if thou swear'st,

    Thou mayst prove false; at lovers' perjuries

    Then say, Jove laughs. O gentle Romeo,

    If thou dost love, pronounce it faithfully:

    Or if thou think'st I am too quickly won,

I'll frown and be perverse an say thee nay,
So thou wilt woo; but else, not for the world.
In truth, fair Montague, I am too fond,
And therefore thou mayst think my 'havior
    light:
But trust me, gentleman, I'll prove more true
Than those that have more cunning to be
    strange.
I should have been more strange, I must
    confess,
But that thou overheard'st, ere I was ware,
My true love's passion: therefore pardon me,
And not impute this yielding to light love,
Which the dark night hath so discovered.

ROMEO

Lady, by yonder blessed moon I swear
That tips with silver all these fruit-tree tops—

JULIET

O, swear not by the moon, the inconstant
    moon,
That monthly changes in her circled orb,
Lest that thy love prove likewise variable.

ROMEO

What shall I swear by?

JULIET

Do not swear at all;
Or, if thou wilt, swear by thy gracious self,

Which is the god of my idolatry,
And I'll believe thee.

ROMEO

If my heart's dear love—

JULIET

Well, do not swear: although I joy in thee,
I have no joy of this contract to-night:
It is too rash, too unadvised, too sudden;
Too like the lightning, which doth cease to be
Ere one can say 'It lightens.' Sweet, good
      night!
This bud of love, by summer's ripening breath,
May prove a beauteous flower when next we
      meet.
Good night, good night! as sweet repose and
      rest
Come to thy heart as that within my breast!

ROMEO

O, wilt thou leave me so unsatisfied?

JULIET

What satisfaction canst thou have to-night?

ROMEO

The exchange of thy love's faithful vow for
mine.

JULIET

I gave thee mine before thou didst request it:
And yet I would it were to give again.

ROMEO

Wouldst thou withdraw it? for what purpose, love?

JULIET

But to be frank, and give it thee again.
And yet I wish but for the thing I have:
My bounty is as boundless as the sea,
My love as deep; the more I give to thee,
The more I have, for both are infinite.
Nurse calls within
I hear some noise within; dear love, adieu!
Anon, good nurse! Sweet Montague, be true.
Stay but a little, I will come again.

Exit, above

ROMEO

O blessed, blessed night! I am afeard.
Being in night, all this is but a dream,
Too flattering-sweet to be substantial.

Re-enter JULIET, above

JULIET

Three words, dear Romeo, and good night indeed.
If that thy bent of love be honourable,
Thy purpose marriage, send me word to-morrow,
By one that I'll procure to come to thee,

Where and what time thou wilt perform the rite;
And all my fortunes at thy foot I'll lay
And follow thee my lord throughout the
        world.

NURSE
    (Within) Madam!

JULIET
    I come, anon.—But if thou mean'st not well,
    I do beseech thee—

NURSE
    (Within) Madam!

JULIET
    By and by, I come:—
    To cease thy suit, and leave me to my grief:
    To-morrow will I send.

ROMEO
    So thrive my soul—

JULIET
    A thousand times good night!

                                        Exit, above

ROMEO
    A thousand times the worse, to want thy light.
    Love goes toward love, as schoolboys from
        their books,
    But love from love, toward school with heavy
        looks.
    Retiring

Re-enter JULIET, above

JULIET

    Hist! Romeo, hist! O, for a falconer's voice,

    To lure this tassel-gentle back again!

    Bondage is hoarse, and may not speak aloud;

    Else would I tear the cave where Echo lies,

    And make her airy tongue more hoarse than
        mine,

    With repetition of my Romeo's name.

ROMEO

    It is my soul that calls upon my name:

    How silver-sweet sound lovers' tongues by
        night,

    Like softest music to attending ears!

JULIET

    Romeo!

ROMEO

    My dear?

JULIET

    At what o'clock to-morrow

    Shall I send to thee?

ROMEO

    At the hour of nine.

JULIET

    I will not fail: 'tis twenty years till then.

    I have forgot why I did call thee back.

ROMEO

Let me stand here till thou remember it.

JULIET

I shall forget, to have thee still stand there,
Remembering how I love thy company.

ROMEO

And I'll still stay, to have thee still forget,
Forgetting any other home but this.

JULIET

'Tis almost morning; I would have thee gone:
And yet no further than a wanton's bird;
Who lets it hop a little from her hand,
Like a poor prisoner in his twisted gyves,
And with a silk thread plucks it back again,
So loving-jealous of his liberty.

ROMEO

I would I were thy bird.

JULIET

Sweet, so would I:
Yet I should kill thee with much cherishing.
Good night, good night! parting is such sweet
    sorrow,
That I shall say good night till it be morrow.

Exit above

ROMEO

Sleep dwell upon thine eyes, peace in thy
    breast!

Would I were sleep and peace, so sweet to rest!
Hence will I to my ghostly father's cell,
His help to crave, and my dear hap to tell.

Exit

SCENE III. FRIAR LAURENCE'S CELL.

Enter FRIAR LAURENCE, with a basket
FRIAR LAURENCE

The grey-eyed morn smiles on the frowning
night,
Chequering the eastern clouds with streaks of
light,
And flecked darkness like a drunkard reels
From forth day's path and Titan's fiery wheels:
Now, ere the sun advance his burning eye,
The day to cheer and night's dank dew to dry,
I must up-fill this osier cage of ours
With baleful weeds and precious-juiced
flowers.
The earth that's nature's mother is her tomb;
What is her burying grave that is her womb,
And from her womb children of divers kind
We sucking on her natural bosom find,
Many for many virtues excellent,
None but for some and yet all different.
O, mickle is the powerful grace that lies

In herbs, plants, stones, and their true qualities:
For nought so vile that on the earth doth live
But to the earth some special good doth give,
Nor aught so good but strain'd from that fair
    use
Revolts from true birth, stumbling on abuse:
Virtue itself turns vice, being misapplied;
And vice sometimes by action dignified.
Within the infant rind of this small flower
Poison hath residence and medicine power:
For this, being smelt, with that part cheers
    each part;
Being tasted, slays all senses with the heart.
Two such opposed kings encamp them still
In man as well as herbs, grace and rude will;
And where the worser is predominant,
Full soon the canker death eats up that plant.

Enter ROMEO
ROMEO
    Good morrow, father.
FRIAR LAURENCE
    Benedicite!
    What early tongue so sweet saluteth me?
    Young son, it argues a distemper'd head
    So soon to bid good morrow to thy bed:
    Care keeps his watch in every old man's eye,

And where care lodges, sleep will never lie;
But where unbruised youth with unstuff'd
    brain
Doth couch his limbs, there golden sleep doth
    reign:
Therefore thy earliness doth me assure
Thou art up-roused by some distemperature;
Or if not so, then here I hit it right,
Our Romeo hath not been in bed to-night.

ROMEO

That last is true; the sweeter rest was mine.

FRIAR LAURENCE

God pardon sin! wast thou with Rosaline?

ROMEO

With Rosaline, my ghostly father? no;
I have forgot that name, and that name's woe.

FRIAR LAURENCE

That's my good son: but where hast thou been,
then?

ROMEO

I'll tell thee, ere thou ask it me again.
I have been feasting with mine enemy,
Where on a sudden one hath wounded me,
That's by me wounded: both our remedies
Within thy help and holy physic lies:
I bear no hatred, blessed man, for, lo,
My intercession likewise steads my foe.

FRIAR LAURENCE

> Be plain, good son, and homely in thy drift;
> Riddling confession finds but riddling shrift.

ROMEO

> Then plainly know my heart's dear love is set
> On the fair daughter of rich Capulet:
> As mine on hers, so hers is set on mine;
> And all combined, save what thou must
> > combine
> By holy marriage: when and where and how
> We met, we woo'd and made exchange of
> > vow,
> I'll tell thee as we pass; but this I pray,
> That thou consent to marry us to-day.

FRIAR LAURENCE

> Holy Saint Francis, what a change is here!
> Is Rosaline, whom thou didst love so dear,
> So soon forsaken? young men's love then lies
> Not truly in their hearts, but in their eyes.
> Jesu Maria, what a deal of brine
> Hath wash'd thy sallow cheeks for Rosaline!
> How much salt water thrown away in waste,
> To season love, that of it doth not taste!
> The sun not yet thy sighs from heaven clears,
> Thy old groans ring yet in my ancient ears;
> Lo, here upon thy cheek the stain doth sit
> Of an old tear that is not wash'd off yet:

If e'er thou wast thyself and these woes thine,
Thou and these woes were all for Rosaline:
And art thou changed? pronounce this sentence
    then,
Women may fall, when there's no strength in
    men.

ROMEO

Thou chid'st me oft for loving Rosaline.

FRIAR LAURENCE

For doting, not for loving, pupil mine.

ROMEO

And bad'st me bury love.

FRIAR LAURENCE

Not in a grave,
To lay one in, another out to have.

ROMEO

I pray thee, chide not; she whom I love now
Doth grace for grace and love for love allow;
The other did not so.

FRIAR LAURENCE

O, she knew well
Thy love did read by rote and could not spell.
But come, young waverer, come, go with me,
In one respect I'll thy assistant be;
For this alliance may so happy prove,
To turn your households' rancour to pure love.

ROMEO

    O, let us hence; I stand on sudden haste.

FRIAR LAURENCE

    Wisely and slow; they stumble that run fast.

Exeunt

SCENE IV. A STREET.

Enter BENVOLIO and MERCUTIO

MERCUTIO

    Where the devil should this Romeo be?

    Came he not home to-night?

BENVOLIO

    Not to his father's; I spoke with his man.

MERCUTIO

    Ah, that same pale hard-hearted wench, that

        Rosaline.

    Torments him so, that he will sure run mad.

BENVOLIO

    Tybalt, the kinsman of old Capulet,

    Hath sent a letter to his father's house.

MERCUTIO

    A challenge, on my life.

BENVOLIO

    Romeo will answer it.

MERCUTIO

    Any man that can write may answer a letter.

BENVOLIO

Nay, he will answer the letter's master, how he dares, being dared.

MERCUTIO

Alas poor Romeo! he is already dead; stabbed with a white wench's black eye; shot through the ear with a love-song; the very pin of his heart cleft with the blind bow-boy's butt-shaft: and is he a man to encounter Tybalt?

BENVOLIO

Why, what is Tybalt?

MERCUTIO

More than prince of cats, I can tell you. O, he is the courageous captain of compliments. He fights as you sing prick-song, keeps time, distance, and proportion; rests me his minim rest, one, two, and the third in your bosom: the very butcher of a silk button, a duellist, a duellist; a gentleman of the very first house, of the first and second cause: ah, the immortal passado! the punto reverso! the hai!

BENVOLIO

The what?

MERCUTIO

The pox of such antic, lisping, affecting fantasticoes; these new tuners of accents! 'By Jesu, a very good blade! a very tall man! a very good whore!' Why, is not this a lamentable thing, grandsire, that we should be thus afflicted with these strange flies, these fashion-mongers, these perdona-mi's, who stand so much on the new form, that they cannot at ease on the old bench? O, their bones, their bones!

Enter ROMEO

BENVOLIO

Here comes Romeo, here comes Romeo.

MERCUTIO

Without his roe, like a dried herring: flesh, flesh, how art thou fishified! Now is he for the numbers that Petrarch flowed in: Laura to his lady was but a kitchen-wench; marry, she had a better love to be-rhyme her; Dido a dowdy; Cleopatra a gipsy; Helen and Hero hildings and harlots; Thisbe a grey eye or so, but not to the purpose. Signior Romeo, bon jour! there's a French salutation to your French slop. You gave us the counterfeit fairly last night.

ROMEO

Good morrow to you both. What counterfeit did I give you?

MERCUTIO

The ship, sir, the slip; can you not conceive?

ROMEO

Pardon, good Mercutio, my business was great; and in such a case as mine a man may strain courtesy.

MERCUTIO

That's as much as to say, such a case as yours constrains a man to bow in the hams.

ROMEO

Meaning, to court'sy.

MERCUTIO

Thou hast most kindly hit it.

ROMEO

A most courteous exposition.

MERCUTIO

Nay, I am the very pink of courtesy.

ROMEO

Pink for flower.

MERCUTIO

Right.

ROMEO

Why, then is my pump well flowered.

MERCUTIO

Well said: follow me this jest now till thou hast worn out thy pump, that when the single sole of it is worn, the jest may remain after the wearing sole singular.

ROMEO

O single-soled jest, solely singular for the singleness.

MERCUTIO

Come between us, good Benvolio; my wits faint.

ROMEO

Switch and spurs, switch and spurs; or I'll cry a match.

MERCUTIO

Nay, if thy wits run the wild-goose chase, I have done, for thou hast more of the wild-goose in one of thy wits than, I am sure, I have in my whole five: was I with you there for the goose?

ROMEO

Thou wast never with me for any thing when thou wast not there for the goose.

MERCUTIO

I will bite thee by the ear for that jest.

ROMEO

Nay, good goose, bite not.

MERCUTIO

Thy wit is a very bitter sweeting; it is a most sharp sauce.

ROMEO

And is it not well served in to a sweet goose?

MERCUTIO

O here's a wit of cheveril, that stretches from
an inch narrow to an ell broad!

ROMEO

I stretch it out for that word 'broad;' which
added to the goose, proves thee far and wide
a broad goose.

MERCUTIO

Why, is not this better now than groaning
for love? now art thou sociable, now art thou
Romeo; now art thou what thou art, by art as
well as by nature: for this drivelling love is like
a great natural, that runs lolling up and down
to hide his bauble in a hole.

BENVOLIO

Stop there, stop there.

MERCUTIO

Thou desirest me to stop in my tale against the
hair.

BENVOLIO

Thou wouldst else have made thy tale large.

MERCUTIO

O, thou art deceived; I would have made it
short: for I was come to the whole depth of
my tale; and meant, indeed, to occupy the
argument no longer.

ROMEO

Here's goodly gear!

Enter Nurse and PETER

MERCUTIO

A sail, a sail!

BENVOLIO

Two, two; a shirt and a smock.

NURSE

Peter!

PETER

Anon!

NURSE

My fan, Peter.

MERCUTIO

Good Peter, to hide her face; for her fan's the fairer face.

NURSE

God ye good morrow, gentlemen.

MERCUTIO

God ye good den, fair gentlewoman.

NURSE

Is it good den?

MERCUTIO

'Tis no less, I tell you, for the bawdy hand of the dial is now upon the prick of noon.

NURSE

Out upon you! what a man are you!

ROMEO

One, gentlewoman, that God hath made for himself to mar.

NURSE

By my troth, it is well said; 'for himself to mar,' quoth a'? Gentlemen, can any of you tell me where I may find the young Romeo?

ROMEO

I can tell you; but young Romeo will be older when you have found him than he was when you sought him: I am the youngest of that name, for fault of a worse.

NURSE

You say well.

MERCUTIO

Yea, is the worst well? very well took, i' faith; wisely, wisely.

NURSE

If you be he, sir, I desire some confidence with you.

BENVOLIO

She will indite him to some supper.

MERCUTIO

A bawd, a bawd, a bawd! so ho!

ROMEO

What hast thou found?

MERCUTIO

No hare, sir; unless a hare, sir, in a lenten pie, that is something stale and hoar ere it be spent.

Sings

An old hare hoar,

And an old hare hoar,

Is very good meat in lent

But a hare that is hoar

Is too much for a score,

When it hoars ere it be spent.

Romeo, will you come to your father's? We'll to dinner, thither.

ROMEO

I will follow you.

MERCUTIO

Farewell, ancient lady; farewell,

Singing

'lady, lady, lady.'

Exeunt MERCUTIO and BENVOLIO

NURSE

Marry, farewell! I pray you, sir, what saucy merchant was this, that was so full of his ropery?

ROMEO

A gentleman, nurse, that loves to hear himself talk, and will speak more in a minute than he will stand to in a month.

NURSE

An a' speak any thing against me, I'll take him down, an a' were lustier than he is, and twenty such Jacks; and if I cannot, I'll find those that shall. Scurvy knave! I am none of his flirt-gills; I am none of his skains-mates. And thou must stand by too, and suffer every knave to use me at his pleasure?

PETER

I saw no man use you a pleasure; if I had, my weapon should quickly have been out, I warrant you: I dare draw as soon as another man, if I see occasion in a good quarrel, and the law on my side.

NURSE

Now, afore God, I am so vexed, that every part about me quivers. Scurvy knave! Pray you, sir, a word: and as I told you, my young lady bade me inquire you out; what she bade me say, I will keep to myself: but first let me tell ye, if ye should lead her into a fool's paradise, as they say, it were a very gross kind of behavior, as they say: for the gentlewoman is young; and,

therefore, if you should deal double with her,
truly it were an ill thing to be offered to any
gentlewoman, and very weak dealing.

ROMEO

Nurse, commend me to thy lady and mistress.
I protest unto thee—

NURSE

Good heart, and, i' faith, I will tell her as
    much:
Lord, Lord, she will be a joyful woman.

ROMEO

What wilt thou tell her, nurse? thou dost not
mark me.

NURSE

I will tell her, sir, that you do protest; which, as
I take it, is a gentlemanlike offer.

ROMEO

Bid her devise
Some means to come to shrift this afternoon;
And there she shall at Friar Laurence' cell
Be shrived and married. Here is for thy pains.

NURSE

No truly sir; not a penny.

ROMEO

Go to; I say you shall.

NURSE

This afternoon, sir? well, she shall be there.

ROMEO

> And stay, good nurse, behind the abbey wall:
> Within this hour my man shall be with thee
> And bring thee cords made like a tackled
>   stair;
> Which to the high top-gallant of my joy
> Must be my convoy in the secret night.
> Farewell; be trusty, and I'll quit thy pains:
> Farewell; commend me to thy mistress.

NURSE

> Now God in heaven bless thee! Hark you, sir.

ROMEO

> What say'st thou, my dear nurse?

NURSE

> Is your man secret? Did you ne'er hear say,
> Two may keep counsel, putting one away?

ROMEO

> I warrant thee, my man's as true as steel.

NURSE

> Well, sir; my mistress is the sweetest lady—
> Lord, Lord! when 'twas a little prating
> thing:—O, there is a nobleman in town, one
> Paris, that would fain lay knife aboard; but she,
> good soul, had as lief see a toad, a very toad,
> as see him. I anger her sometimes and tell her
> that Paris is the properer man; but, I'll warrant
> you, when I say so, she looks as pale as any

clout in the versal world. Doth not rosemary
and Romeo begin both with a letter?

ROMEO

Ay, nurse; what of that? both with an R.

NURSE

Ah. mocker! that's the dog's name; R is for
the—No; I know it begins with some other
letter:—and she hath the prettiest sententious
of it, of you and rosemary, that it would do you
good to hear it.

ROMEO

Commend me to thy lady.

NURSE

Ay, a thousand times.

Exit Romeo

Peter!

PETER

Anon!

NURSE

Peter, take my fan, and go before and apace.

Exeunt

SCENE V. CAPULET'S ORCHARD.

Enter JULIET

JULIET

The clock struck nine when I did send the
  nurse;
In half an hour she promised to return.
Perchance she cannot meet him: that's not so.
O, she is lame! love's heralds should be
  thoughts,
Which ten times faster glide than the sun's
  beams,
Driving back shadows over louring hills:
Therefore do nimble-pinion'd doves draw love,
And therefore hath the wind-swift Cupid
  wings.
Now is the sun upon the highmost hill
Of this day's journey, and from nine till twelve
Is three long hours, yet she is not come.
Had she affections and warm youthful blood,
She would be as swift in motion as a ball;
My words would bandy her to my sweet love,
And his to me:
But old folks, many feign as they were dead;
Unwieldy, slow, heavy and pale as lead.
O God, she comes!

Enter Nurse and PETER

O honey nurse, what news?

Hast thou met with him? Send thy man away.

NURSE

Peter, stay at the gate.

Exit PETER

JULIET

Now, good sweet nurse,—O Lord, why look'st
thou sad?

Though news be sad, yet tell them merrily;

If good, thou shamest the music of sweet news

By playing it to me with so sour a face.

NURSE

I am a-weary, give me leave awhile:

Fie, how my bones ache! what a jaunt have I
had!

JULIET

I would thou hadst my bones, and I thy news:

Nay, come, I pray thee, speak; good, good nurse,
speak.

NURSE

Jesu, what haste? can you not stay awhile?

Do you not see that I am out of breath?

JULIET

How art thou out of breath, when thou hast
breath

To say to me that thou art out of breath?

The excuse that thou dost make in this delay
Is longer than the tale thou dost excuse.
Is thy news good, or bad? answer to that;
Say either, and I'll stay the circumstance:
Let me be satisfied, is't good or bad?

NURSE

Well, you have made a simple choice; you know
not how to choose a man: Romeo! no, not he;
though his face be better than any man's, yet
his leg excels all men's; and for a hand, and
a foot, and a body, though they be not to be
talked on, yet they are past compare: he is not
the flower of courtesy, but, I'll warrant him, as
gentle as a lamb. Go thy ways, wench; serve
God. What, have you dined at home?

JULIET

No, no: but all this did I know before.
What says he of our marriage? what of that?

NURSE

Lord, how my head aches! what a head have I!
It beats as it would fall in twenty pieces.
My back o' t' other side,—O, my back, my
      back!
Beshrew your heart for sending me about,
To catch my death with jaunting up and down!

JULIET

I' faith, I am sorry that thou art not well.

Sweet, sweet, sweet nurse, tell me, what says
    my love?

NURSE

Your love says, like an honest gentleman, and
a courteous, and a kind, and a handsome, and,
I warrant, a virtuous,—Where is your mother?

JULIET

Where is my mother! why, she is within;
Where should she be? How oddly thou repliest!
'Your love says, like an honest gentleman,
Where is your mother?'

NURSE

O God's lady dear!
Are you so hot? marry, come up, I trow;
Is this the poultice for my aching bones?
Henceforward do your messages yourself.

JULIET

Here's such a coil! come, what says Romeo?

NURSE

Have you got leave to go to shrift to-day?

JULIET

I have.

NURSE

Then hie you hence to Friar Laurence' cell;
There stays a husband to make you a wife:
Now comes the wanton blood up in your
    cheeks,

They'll be in scarlet straight at any news.
Hie you to church; I must another way,
To fetch a ladder, by the which your love
Must climb a bird's nest soon when it is dark:
I am the drudge and toil in your delight,
But you shall bear the burden soon at night.
Go; I'll to dinner: hie you to the cell.

JULIET

Hie to high fortune! Honest nurse, farewell.

Exeunt

SCENE VI. FRIAR LAURENCE'S CELL.

Enter FRIAR LAURENCE and ROMEO

FRIAR LAURENCE

So smile the heavens upon this holy act,
That after hours with sorrow chide us not!

ROMEO

Amen, amen! but come what sorrow can,
It cannot countervail the exchange of joy
That one short minute gives me in her sight:
Do thou but close our hands with holy words,
Then love-devouring death do what he dare;
It is enough I may but call her mine.

FRIAR LAURENCE

These violent delights have violent ends
And in their triumph die, like fire and powder,

Which as they kiss consume: the sweetest honey
Is loathsome in his own deliciousness
And in the taste confounds the appetite:
Therefore love moderately; long love doth so;
Too swift arrives as tardy as too slow.

Enter JULIET

Here comes the lady: O, so light a foot
Will ne'er wear out the everlasting flint:
A lover may bestride the gossamer
That idles in the wanton summer air,
And yet not fall; so light is vanity.

JULIET

Good even to my ghostly confessor.

FRIAR LAURENCE

Romeo shall thank thee, daughter, for us both.

JULIET

As much to him, else is his thanks too much.

ROMEO

Ah, Juliet, if the measure of thy joy
Be heap'd like mine and that thy skill be more
To blazon it, then sweeten with thy breath
This neighbour air, and let rich music's tongue
Unfold the imagined happiness that both
Receive in either by this dear encounter.

JULIET

Conceit, more rich in matter than in words,

Brags of his substance, not of ornament:
They are but beggars that can count their worth;
But my true love is grown to such excess
I cannot sum up sum of half my wealth.

FRIAR LAURENCE
Come, come with me, and we will make short
work;
For, by your leaves, you shall not stay alone
Till holy church incorporate two in one.

Exeunt

Act 3

SCENE I. A PUBLIC PLACE.

Enter MERCUTIO, BENVOLIO, Page, and Servants

BENVOLIO

    I pray thee, good Mercutio, let's retire:

    The day is hot, the Capulets abroad,

    And, if we meet, we shall not scape a brawl;

    For now, these hot days, is the mad blood

        stirring.

MERCUTIO

    Thou art like one of those fellows that when
he enters the confines of a tavern claps me
his sword upon the table and says 'God send
me no need of thee!' and by the operation of
the second cup draws it on the drawer, when
indeed there is no need.

BENVOLIO

Am I like such a fellow?

MERCUTIO

Come, come, thou art as hot a Jack in thy mood as any in Italy, and as soon moved to be moody, and as soon moody to be moved.

BENVOLIO

And what to?

MERCUTIO

Nay, an there were two such, we should have none shortly, for one would kill the other. Thou! why, thou wilt quarrel with a man that hath a hair more, or a hair less, in his beard, than thou hast: thou wilt quarrel with a man for cracking nuts, having no other reason but because thou hast hazel eyes: what eye but such an eye would spy out such a quarrel? Thy head is as fun of quarrels as an egg is full of meat, and yet thy head hath been beaten as addle as an egg for quarrelling: thou hast quarrelled with a man for coughing in the street, because he hath wakened thy dog that hath lain asleep in the sun: didst thou not fall out with a tailor for wearing his new doublet before Easter? with another, for tying his new shoes with old riband? and yet thou wilt tutor me from quarrelling!

BENVOLIO

> An I were so apt to quarrel as thou art, any
> man should buy the fee-simple of my life for
> an hour and a quarter.

MERCUTIO

> The fee-simple! O simple!

BENVOLIO

> By my head, here come the Capulets.

MERCUTIO

> By my heel, I care not.

Enter TYBALT and others

TYBALT

> Follow me close, for I will speak to them.
> Gentlemen, good den: a word with one of you.

MERCUTIO

> And but one word with one of us? couple it
> with something; make it a word and a blow.

TYBALT

> You shall find me apt enough to that, sir, an
> you will give me occasion.

MERCUTIO

> Could you not take some occasion without
> giving?

TYBALT

> Mercutio, thou consort'st with Romeo,—

MERCUTIO

Consort! what, dost thou make us minstrels?
an thou make minstrels of us, look to hear
nothing but discords: here's my fiddlestick;
here's that shall make you dance. 'Zounds,
consort!

BENVOLIO

We talk here in the public haunt of men:
Either withdraw unto some private place,
And reason coldly of your grievances,
Or else depart; here all eyes gaze on us.

MERCUTIO

Men's eyes were made to look, and let them
  gaze;
I will not budge for no man's pleasure, I.

Enter ROMEO

TYBALT

Well, peace be with you, sir: here comes my
man.

MERCUTIO

But I'll be hanged, sir, if he wear your livery:
Marry, go before to field, he'll be your follower;
Your worship in that sense may call him 'man.'

TYBALT

Romeo, the hate I bear thee can afford
No better term than this,—thou art a villain.

ROMEO

    Tybalt, the reason that I have to love thee

    Doth much excuse the appertaining rage

    To such a greeting: villain am I none;

    Therefore farewell; I see thou know'st me not.

TYBALT

    Boy, this shall not excuse the injuries

    That thou hast done me; therefore turn and

        draw.

ROMEO

    I do protest, I never injured thee,

    But love thee better than thou canst devise,

    Till thou shalt know the reason of my love:

    And so, good Capulet,—which name I tender

    As dearly as my own,—be satisfied.

MERCUTIO

    O calm, dishonourable, vile submission!

    Alla stoccata carries it away.

    Draws

    Tybalt, you rat-catcher, will you walk?

TYBALT

    What wouldst thou have with me?

MERCUTIO

    Good king of cats, nothing but one of your
nine lives; that I mean to make bold withal,
and as you shall use me hereafter, drybeat the
rest of the eight. Will you pluck your sword out

of his pitcher by the ears? make haste, lest mine
be about your ears ere it be out.

TYBALT

I am for you.

Drawing

ROMEO

Gentle Mercutio, put thy rapier up.

MERCUTIO

Come, sir, your passado.

They fight

ROMEO

Draw, Benvolio; beat down their weapons.
Gentlemen, for shame, forbear this outrage!
Tybalt, Mercutio, the prince expressly hath
Forbidden bandying in Verona streets:
Hold, Tybalt! good Mercutio!

*TYBALT under ROMEO's arm stabs MERCUTIO,
and flies with his followers*

MERCUTIO

I am hurt.
A plague o' both your houses! I am sped.
Is he gone, and hath nothing?

BENVOLIO

What, art thou hurt?

MERCUTIO

Ay, ay, a scratch, a scratch; marry, 'tis enough.

Where is my page? Go, villain, fetch a surgeon.

Exit Page

ROMEO

Courage, man; the hurt cannot be much.

MERCUTIO

No, 'tis not so deep as a well, nor so wide as a church-door; but 'tis enough, 'twill serve: ask for me to-morrow, and you shall find me a grave man. I am peppered, I warrant, for this world. A plague o' both your houses! 'Zounds, a dog, a rat, a mouse, a cat, to scratch a man to death! a braggart, a rogue, a villain, that fights by the book of arithmetic! Why the devil came you between us? I was hurt under your arm.

ROMEO

I thought all for the best.

MERCUTIO

Help me into some house, Benvolio,
Or I shall faint. A plague o' both your houses!
They have made worms' meat of me: I have it,
And soundly too: your houses!

Exeunt MERCUTIO and BENVOLIO

ROMEO

This gentleman, the prince's near ally,
My very friend, hath got his mortal hurt
In my behalf; my reputation stain'd
With Tybalt's slander,—Tybalt, that an hour

Hath been my kinsman! O sweet Juliet,
Thy beauty hath made me effeminate
And in my temper soften'd valour's steel!

Re-enter BENVOLIO
BENVOLIO
O Romeo, Romeo, brave Mercutio's dead!
That gallant spirit hath aspired the clouds,
Which too untimely here did scorn the earth.
ROMEO
This day's black fate on more days doth
    depend;
This but begins the woe, others must end.
BENVOLIO
Here comes the furious Tybalt back again.
ROMEO
Alive, in triumph! and Mercutio slain!
Away to heaven, respective lenity,
And fire-eyed fury be my conduct now!

Re-enter TYBALT
Now, Tybalt, take the villain back again,
That late thou gavest me; for Mercutio's soul
Is but a little way above our heads,
Staying for thine to keep him company:
Either thou, or I, or both, must go with him.

TYBALT

Thou, wretched boy, that didst consort him
here, Shalt with him hence.

ROMEO

This shall determine that.

They fight; TYBALT falls

BENVOLIO

Romeo, away, be gone!

The citizens are up, and Tybalt slain.

Stand not amazed: the prince will doom thee
death,

If thou art taken: hence, be gone, away!

ROMEO

O, I am fortune's fool!

BENVOLIO

Why dost thou stay?

Exit ROMEO

Enter Citizens, & c

FIRST CITIZEN

Which way ran he that kill'd Mercutio?

Tybalt, that murderer, which way ran he?

BENVOLIO

There lies that Tybalt.

FIRST CITIZEN

Up, sir, go with me;

I charge thee in the princes name, obey.

Enter Prince, attended; MONTAGUE, CAPULET,
their Wives, and others

PRINCE

Where are the vile beginners of this fray?

BENVOLIO

O noble prince, I can discover all
The unlucky manage of this fatal brawl:
There lies the man, slain by young Romeo,
That slew thy kinsman, brave Mercutio.

LADY CAPULET

Tybalt, my cousin! O my brother's child!
O prince! O cousin! husband! O, the blood is
spilt
O my dear kinsman! Prince, as thou art true,
For blood of ours, shed blood of Montague.
O cousin, cousin!

PRINCE

Benvolio, who began this bloody fray?

BENVOLIO

Tybalt, here slain, whom Romeo's hand did slay;
Romeo that spoke him fair, bade him bethink
How nice the quarrel was, and urged withal
Your high displeasure: all this uttered
With gentle breath, calm look, knees humbly
bow'd,
Could not take truce with the unruly spleen
Of Tybalt deaf to peace, but that he tilts

With piercing steel at bold Mercutio's breast,
Who all as hot, turns deadly point to point,
And, with a martial scorn, with one hand beats
Cold death aside, and with the other sends
It back to Tybalt, whose dexterity,
Retorts it: Romeo he cries aloud,
'Hold, friends! friends, part!' and, swifter than
    his tongue,
His agile arm beats down their fatal points,
And 'twixt them rushes; underneath whose
    arm
An envious thrust from Tybalt hit the life
Of stout Mercutio, and then Tybalt fled;
But by and by comes back to Romeo,
Who had but newly entertain'd revenge,
And to't they go like lightning, for, ere I
Could draw to part them, was stout Tybalt
    slain.
And, as he fell, did Romeo turn and fly.
This is the truth, or let Benvolio die.

LADY CAPULET

He is a kinsman to the Montague;
Affection makes him false; he speaks not true:
Some twenty of them fought in this black strife,
And all those twenty could but kill one life.
I beg for justice, which thou, prince, must give;
Romeo slew Tybalt, Romeo must not live.

PRINCE

Romeo slew him, he slew Mercutio;
Who now the price of his dear blood doth
owe?

MONTAGUE

Not Romeo, prince, he was Mercutio's friend;
His fault concludes but what the law should
end,
The life of Tybalt.

PRINCE

And for that offence
Immediately we do exile him hence:
I have an interest in your hate's proceeding,
My blood for your rude brawls doth lie
a-bleeding;
But I'll amerce you with so strong a fine
That you shall all repent the loss of mine:
I will be deaf to pleading and excuses;
Nor tears nor prayers shall purchase out
abuses:
Therefore use none: let Romeo hence in haste,
Else, when he's found, that hour is his last.
Bear hence this body and attend our will:
Mercy but murders, pardoning those that kill.

Exeunt

SCENE II. CAPULET'S ORCHARD.

Enter JULIET
JULIET
    Gallop apace, you fiery-footed steeds,
    Towards Phoebus' lodging: such a wagoner
    As Phaethon would whip you to the west,
    And bring in cloudy night immediately.
    Spread thy close curtain, love-performing night,
    That runaway's eyes may wink and Romeo
    Leap to these arms, untalk'd of and unseen.
    Lovers can see to do their amorous rites
    By their own beauties; or, if love be blind,
    It best agrees with night. Come, civil night,
    Thou sober-suited matron, all in black,
    And learn me how to lose a winning match,
    Play'd for a pair of stainless maidenhoods:
    Hood my unmann'd blood, bating in my cheeks,
    With thy black mantle; till strange love, grown
        bold,
    Think true love acted simple modesty.
    Come, night; come, Romeo; come, thou day in
        night;
    For thou wilt lie upon the wings of night
    Whiter than new snow on a raven's back.
    Come, gentle night, come, loving, black-brow'd
        night,

Give me my Romeo; and, when he shall die,
Take him and cut him out in little stars,
And he will make the face of heaven so fine
That all the world will be in love with night
And pay no worship to the garish sun.
O, I have bought the mansion of a love,
But not possess'd it, and, though I am sold,
Not yet enjoy'd: so tedious is this day
As is the night before some festival
To an impatient child that hath new robes
And may not wear them. O, here comes my
    nurse,
And she brings news; and every tongue that
    speaks
But Romeo's name speaks heavenly eloquence.

Enter Nurse, with cords

Now, nurse, what news? What hast thou there?
the cords That Romeo bid thee fetch?

NURSE

Ay, ay, the cords.

Throws them down

JULIET

Ay me! what news? why dost thou wring thy
hands?

NURSE

Ah, well-a-day! he's dead, he's dead, he's dead!

We are undone, lady, we are undone!
Alack the day! he's gone, he's kill'd, he's dead!

JULIET

Can heaven be so envious?

NURSE

Romeo can,
Though heaven cannot: O Romeo, Romeo!
Who ever would have thought it? Romeo!

JULIET

What devil art thou, that dost torment me thus?
This torture should be roar'd in dismal hell.
Hath Romeo slain himself? say thou but 'I,'
And that bare vowel 'I' shall poison more
Than the death-darting eye of cockatrice:
I am not I, if there be such an I;
Or those eyes shut, that make thee answer 'I.'
If he be slain, say 'I'; or if not, no:
Brief sounds determine of my weal or woe.

NURSE

I saw the wound, I saw it with mine eyes,—
God save the mark!—here on his manly breast:
A piteous corse, a bloody piteous corse;
Pale, pale as ashes, all bedaub'd in blood,
All in gore-blood; I swounded at the sight.

JULIET

O, break, my heart! poor bankrupt, break at
    once!

To prison, eyes, ne'er look on liberty!

Vile earth, to earth resign; end motion here;

And thou and Romeo press one heavy bier!

NURSE

O Tybalt, Tybalt, the best friend I had!

O courteous Tybalt! honest gentleman!

That ever I should live to see thee dead!

JULIET

What storm is this that blows so contrary?

Is Romeo slaughter'd, and is Tybalt dead?

My dear-loved cousin, and my dearer lord?

Then, dreadful trumpet, sound the general
doom!

For who is living, if those two are gone?

NURSE

Tybalt is gone, and Romeo banished;

Romeo that kill'd him, he is banished.

JULIET

O God! did Romeo's hand shed Tybalt's blood?

NURSE

It did, it did; alas the day, it did!

JULIET

O serpent heart, hid with a flowering face!

Did ever dragon keep so fair a cave?

Beautiful tyrant! fiend angelical!

Dove-feather'd raven! wolvish-ravening lamb!

Despised substance of divinest show!

Just opposite to what thou justly seem'st,
A damned saint, an honourable villain!
O nature, what hadst thou to do in hell,
When thou didst bower the spirit of a fiend
In moral paradise of such sweet flesh?
Was ever book containing such vile matter
So fairly bound? O that deceit should dwell
In such a gorgeous palace!

NURSE

There's no trust,
No faith, no honesty in men; all perjured,
All forsworn, all naught, all dissemblers.
Ah, where's my man? give me some aqua vitae:
These griefs, these woes, these sorrows make
    me old.
Shame come to Romeo!

JULIET

Blister'd be thy tongue
For such a wish! he was not born to shame:
Upon his brow shame is ashamed to sit;
For 'tis a throne where honour may be crown'd
Sole monarch of the universal earth.
O, what a beast was I to chide at him!

NURSE

Will you speak well of him that kill'd your
cousin?

JULIET

Shall I speak ill of him that is my husband?
Ah, poor my lord, what tongue shall smooth
 thy name,
When I, thy three-hours wife, have mangled it?
But, wherefore, villain, didst thou kill my cousin?
That villain cousin would have kill'd my
 husband:
Back, foolish tears, back to your native spring;
Your tributary drops belong to woe,
Which you, mistaking, offer up to joy.
My husband lives, that Tybalt would have slain;
And Tybalt's dead, that would have slain my
 husband:
All this is comfort; wherefore weep I then?
Some word there was, worser than Tybalt's death,
That murder'd me: I would forget it fain;
But, O, it presses to my memory,
Like damned guilty deeds to sinners' minds:
'Tybalt is dead, and Romeo—banished;'
That 'banished,' that one word 'banished,'
Hath slain ten thousand Tybalts. Tybalt's death
Was woe enough, if it had ended there:
Or, if sour woe delights in fellowship
And needly will be rank'd with other griefs,
Why follow'd not, when she said 'Tybalt's
 dead,'

Thy father, or thy mother, nay, or both,
Which modern lamentations might have
    moved?
But with a rear-ward following Tybalt's death,
'Romeo is banished,' to speak that word,
Is father, mother, Tybalt, Romeo, Juliet,
All slain, all dead. 'Romeo is banished!'
There is no end, no limit, measure, bound,
In that word's death; no words can that woe
    sound.
Where is my father, and my mother, nurse?

NURSE

Weeping and wailing over Tybalt's corse:
Will you go to them? I will bring you thither.

JULIET

Wash they his wounds with tears: mine shall
    be spent,
When theirs are dry, for Romeo's banishment.
Take up those cords: poor ropes, you are
    beguiled,
Both you and I; for Romeo is exiled:
He made you for a highway to my bed;
But I, a maid, die maiden-widowed.
Come, cords, come, nurse; I'll to my wedding-
    bed;
And death, not Romeo, take my maidenhead!

NURSE

Hie to your chamber: I'll find Romeo
To comfort you: I wot well where he is.
Hark ye, your Romeo will be here at night:
I'll to him; he is hid at Laurence' cell.

JULIET

O, find him! give this ring to my true knight,
And bid him come to take his last farewell.

Exeunt

SCENE III. FRIAR LAURENCE'S CELL.

Enter FRIAR LAURENCE

FRIAR LAURENCE

Romeo, come forth; come forth, thou fearful
man:
Affliction is enamour'd of thy parts,
And thou art wedded to calamity.

Enter ROMEO

ROMEO

Father, what news? what is the prince's doom?
What sorrow craves acquaintance at my hand,
That I yet know not?

FRIAR LAURENCE

Too familiar

Is my dear son with such sour company:

I bring thee tidings of the prince's doom.

ROMEO

What less than dooms-day is the prince's doom?

FRIAR LAURENCE

A gentler judgment vanish'd from his lips,

Not body's death, but body's banishment.

ROMEO

Ha, banishment! be merciful, say 'death;'

For exile hath more terror in his look,

Much more than death: do not say 'banishment.'

FRIAR LAURENCE

Hence from Verona art thou banished:

Be patient, for the world is broad and wide.

ROMEO

There is no world without Verona walls,

But purgatory, torture, hell itself.

Hence-banished is banish'd from the world,

And world's exile is death: then banished,

Is death mis-term'd: calling death banishment,

Thou cutt'st my head off with a golden axe,

And smilest upon the stroke that murders me.

FRIAR LAURENCE

O deadly sin! O rude unthankfulness!

Thy fault our law calls death; but the kind prince,

Taking thy part, hath rush'd aside the law,
And turn'd that black word death to banishment:
This is dear mercy, and thou seest it not.

ROMEO

'Tis torture, and not mercy: heaven is here,
Where Juliet lives; and every cat and dog
And little mouse, every unworthy thing,
Live here in heaven and may look on her;
But Romeo may not: more validity,
More honourable state, more courtship lives
In carrion-flies than Romeo: they my seize
On the white wonder of dear Juliet's hand
And steal immortal blessing from her lips,
Who even in pure and vestal modesty,
Still blush, as thinking their own kisses sin;
But Romeo may not; he is banished:
Flies may do this, but I from this must fly:
They are free men, but I am banished.
And say'st thou yet that exile is not death?
Hadst thou no poison mix'd, no sharp-ground
        knife,
No sudden mean of death, though ne'er so
        mean,
But 'banished' to kill me?—'banished'?
O friar, the damned use that word in hell;
Howlings attend it: how hast thou the heart,
Being a divine, a ghostly confessor,

A sin-absolver, and my friend profess'd,
To mangle me with that word 'banished'?

FRIAR LAURENCE

Thou fond mad man, hear me but speak a
word.

ROMEO

O, thou wilt speak again of banishment.

FRIAR LAURENCE

I'll give thee armour to keep off that word:
Adversity's sweet milk, philosophy,
To comfort thee, though thou art banished.

ROMEO

Yet 'banished'? Hang up philosophy!
Unless philosophy can make a Juliet,
Displant a town, reverse a prince's doom,
It helps not, it prevails not: talk no more.

FRIAR LAURENCE

O, then I see that madmen have no ears.

ROMEO

How should they, when that wise men have no
eyes?

FRIAR LAURENCE

Let me dispute with thee of thy estate.

ROMEO

Thou canst not speak of that thou dost not
feel:
Wert thou as young as I, Juliet thy love,

An hour but married, Tybalt murdered,
Doting like me and like me banished,
Then mightst thou speak, then mightst thou
        tear thy hair,
And fall upon the ground, as I do now,
Taking the measure of an unmade grave.
Knocking within

FRIAR LAURENCE

Arise; one knocks; good Romeo, hide thyself.

ROMEO

Not I; unless the breath of heartsick groans,
Mist-like, infold me from the search of eyes.
Knocking

FRIAR LAURENCE

Hark, how they knock! Who's there? Romeo,
        arise;
Thou wilt be taken. Stay awhile! Stand up;
Knocking
Run to my study. By and by! God's will,
What simpleness is this! I come, I come!
Knocking
Who knocks so hard? whence come you?
what's your will?

NURSE

(Within) Let me come in, and you shall know
        my errand;
I come from Lady Juliet.

FRIAR LAURENCE
  Welcome, then.

Enter Nurse

NURSE
  O holy friar, O, tell me, holy friar,
  Where is my lady's lord, where's Romeo?

FRIAR LAURENCE
  There on the ground, with his own tears made
  drunk.

NURSE
  O, he is even in my mistress' case,
  Just in her case! O woful sympathy!
  Piteous predicament! Even so lies she,
  Blubbering and weeping, weeping and
      blubbering.
  Stand up, stand up; stand, and you be a man:
  For Juliet's sake, for her sake, rise and stand;
  Why should you fall into so deep an O?

ROMEO
  Nurse!

NURSE
  Ah sir! ah sir! Well, death's the end of all.

ROMEO
  Spakest thou of Juliet? how is it with her?
  Doth she not think me an old murderer,
  Now I have stain'd the childhood of our joy

With blood removed but little from her own?
Where is she? and how doth she? and what
says
My conceal'd lady to our cancell'd love?

NURSE

O, she says nothing, sir, but weeps and weeps;
And now falls on her bed; and then starts up,
And Tybalt calls; and then on Romeo cries,
And then down falls again.

ROMEO

As if that name,
Shot from the deadly level of a gun,
Did murder her; as that name's cursed hand
Murder'd her kinsman. O, tell me, friar, tell me,
In what vile part of this anatomy
Doth my name lodge? tell me, that I may sack
The hateful mansion.

Drawing his sword

FRIAR LAURENCE

Hold thy desperate hand:
Art thou a man? thy form cries out thou art:
Thy tears are womanish; thy wild acts denote
The unreasonable fury of a beast:
Unseemly woman in a seeming man!
Or ill-beseeming beast in seeming both!
Thou hast amazed me: by my holy order,
I thought thy disposition better temper'd.

Hast thou slain Tybalt? wilt thou slay thyself?
And stay thy lady too that lives in thee,
By doing damned hate upon thyself?
Why rail'st thou on thy birth, the heaven, and
　　earth?
Since birth, and heaven, and earth, all three do
　　meet
In thee at once; which thou at once wouldst
　　lose.
Fie, fie, thou shamest thy shape, thy love, thy
　　wit;
Which, like a usurer, abound'st in all,
And usest none in that true use indeed
Which should bedeck thy shape, thy love, thy
　　wit:
Thy noble shape is but a form of wax,
Digressing from the valour of a man;
Thy dear love sworn but hollow perjury,
Killing that love which thou hast vow'd to
　　cherish;
Thy wit, that ornament to shape and love,
Misshapen in the conduct of them both,
Like powder in a skitless soldier's flask,
Is set afire by thine own ignorance,
And thou dismember'd with thine own
　　defence.
What, rouse thee, man! thy Juliet is alive,

For whose dear sake thou wast but lately dead;
There art thou happy: Tybalt would kill thee,
But thou slew'st Tybalt; there are thou happy
    too:
The law that threaten'd death becomes thy
    friend
And turns it to exile; there art thou happy:
A pack of blessings lights up upon thy back;
Happiness courts thee in her best array;
But, like a misbehaved and sullen wench,
Thou pout'st upon thy fortune and thy love:
Take heed, take heed, for such die miserable.
Go, get thee to thy love, as was decreed,
Ascend her chamber, hence and comfort her:
But look thou stay not till the watch be set,
For then thou canst not pass to Mantua;
Where thou shalt live, till we can find a time
To blaze your marriage, reconcile your friends,
Beg pardon of the prince, and call thee back
With twenty hundred thousand times more joy
Than thou went'st forth in lamentation.
Go before, nurse: commend me to thy lady;
And bid her hasten all the house to bed,
Which heavy sorrow makes them apt unto:
Romeo is coming.

NURSE

O Lord, I could have stay'd here all the night

To hear good counsel: O, what learning is!
My lord, I'll tell my lady you will come.

ROMEO

Do so, and bid my sweet prepare to chide.

NURSE

Here, sir, a ring she bid me give you, sir:
Hie you, make haste, for it grows very late.

Exit

ROMEO

How well my comfort is revived by this!

FRIAR LAURENCE

Go hence; good night; and here stands all your
state:
Either be gone before the watch be set,
Or by the break of day disguised from hence:
Sojourn in Mantua; I'll find out your man,
And he shall signify from time to time
Every good hap to you that chances here:
Give me thy hand; 'tis late: farewell; good
night.

ROMEO

But that a joy past joy calls out on me,
It were a grief, so brief to part with thee:
Farewell.

Exeunt

SCENE IV. A ROOM IN CAPULET'S HOUSE.

Enter CAPULET, LADY CAPULET, and PARIS

CAPULET

    Things have fall'n out, sir, so unluckily,

    That we have had no time to move our
        daughter:

    Look you, she loved her kinsman Tybalt
        dearly,

    And so did I:—Well, we were born to die.

    'Tis very late, she'll not come down to-night:

    I promise you, but for your company,

    I would have been a-bed an hour ago.

PARIS

    These times of woe afford no time to woo.

    Madam, good night: commend me to your
        daughter.

LADY CAPULET

    I will, and know her mind early to-morrow;

    To-night she is mew'd up to her heaviness.

CAPULET

    Sir Paris, I will make a desperate tender

    Of my child's love: I think she will be ruled

    In all respects by me; nay, more, I doubt it not.

    Wife, go you to her ere you go to bed;

    Acquaint her here of my son Paris' love;

And bid her, mark you me, on Wednesday
    next—
But, soft! what day is this?

PARIS

Monday, my lord,

CAPULET

Monday! ha, ha! Well, Wednesday is too soon,
O' Thursday let it be: o' Thursday, tell her,
She shall be married to this noble earl.
Will you be ready? do you like this haste?
We'll keep no great ado,—a friend or two;
For, hark you, Tybalt being slain so late,
It may be thought we held him carelessly,
Being our kinsman, if we revel much:
Therefore we'll have some half a dozen
    friends,
And there an end. But what say you to
    Thursday?

PARIS

My lord, I would that Thursday were to-
morrow.

CAPULET

Well get you gone: o' Thursday be it, then.
Go you to Juliet ere you go to bed,
Prepare her, wife, against this wedding-day.
Farewell, my lord. Light to my chamber, ho!
Afore me! it is so very very late,

That we may call it early by and by.
Good night.

Exeunt

SCENE V. CAPULET'S ORCHARD.

Enter ROMEO and JULIET above, at the window

JULIET

    Wilt thou be gone? it is not yet near day:
    It was the nightingale, and not the lark,
    That pierced the fearful hollow of thine ear;
    Nightly she sings on yon pomegranate-tree:
    Believe me, love, it was the nightingale.

ROMEO

    It was the lark, the herald of the morn,
    No nightingale: look, love, what envious
        streaks
    Do lace the severing clouds in yonder east:
    Night's candles are burnt out, and jocund day
    Stands tiptoe on the misty mountain tops.
    I must be gone and live, or stay and die.

JULIET

    Yon light is not day-light, I know it, I:
    It is some meteor that the sun exhales,
    To be to thee this night a torch-bearer,
    And light thee on thy way to Mantua:
    Therefore stay yet; thou need'st not to be gone.

ROMEO

 Let me be ta'en, let me be put to death;
 I am content, so thou wilt have it so.
 I'll say yon grey is not the morning's eye,
 'Tis but the pale reflex of Cynthia's brow;
 Nor that is not the lark, whose notes do beat
 The vaulty heaven so high above our heads:
 I have more care to stay than will to go:
 Come, death, and welcome! Juliet wills it so.
 How is't, my soul? let's talk; it is not day.

JULIET

 It is, it is: hie hence, be gone, away!
 It is the lark that sings so out of tune,
 Straining harsh discords and unpleasing
  sharps.
 Some say the lark makes sweet division;
 This doth not so, for she divideth us:
 Some say the lark and loathed toad change
  eyes,
 O, now I would they had changed voices too!
 Since arm from arm that voice doth us affray,
 Hunting thee hence with hunt's-up to the day,
 O, now be gone; more light and light it grows.

ROMEO

 More light and light; more dark and dark our
 woes!

Enter Nurse, to the chamber

NURSE

Madam!

JULIET

Nurse?

NURSE

Your lady mother is coming to your chamber:

The day is broke; be wary, look about.

Exit

JULIET

Then, window, let day in, and let life out.

ROMEO

Farewell, farewell! one kiss, and I'll descend.

He goeth down

JULIET

Art thou gone so? love, lord, ay, husband,
    friend!

I must hear from thee every day in the hour,

For in a minute there are many days:

O, by this count I shall be much in years

Ere I again behold my Romeo!

ROMEO

Farewell!

I will omit no opportunity

That may convey my greetings, love, to thee.

JULIET

O think'st thou we shall ever meet again?

ROMEO

    I doubt it not; and all these woes shall serve

    For sweet discourses in our time to come.

JULIET

    O God, I have an ill-divining soul!

    Methinks I see thee, now thou art below,

    As one dead in the bottom of a tomb:

    Either my eyesight fails, or thou look'st pale.

ROMEO

    And trust me, love, in my eye so do you:

    Dry sorrow drinks our blood. Adieu, adieu!

                           Exit

JULIET

    O fortune, fortune! all men call thee fickle:

    If thou art fickle, what dost thou with him.

    That is renown'd for faith? Be fickle, fortune;

    For then, I hope, thou wilt not keep him long,

    But send him back.

LADY CAPULET

    (Within) Ho, daughter! are you up?

JULIET

    Who is't that calls? is it my lady mother?

    Is she not down so late, or up so early?

    What unaccustom'd cause procures her hither?

Enter LADY CAPULET

LADY CAPULET

Why, how now, Juliet!

JULIET

Madam, I am not well.

LADY CAPULET

Evermore weeping for your cousin's death?

What, wilt thou wash him from his grave with
tears?

An if thou couldst, thou couldst not make him
live;

Therefore, have done: some grief shows much
of love;

But much of grief shows still some want of wit.

JULIET

Yet let me weep for such a feeling loss.

LADY CAPULET

So shall you feel the loss, but not the friend
Which you weep for.

JULIET

Feeling so the loss,

Cannot choose but ever weep the friend.

LADY CAPULET

Well, girl, thou weep'st not so much for his
death,

As that the villain lives which slaughter'd him.

JULIET

What villain madam?

LADY CAPULET

That same villain, Romeo.

JULIET

(Aside) Villain and he be many miles asunder.—

God Pardon him! I do, with all my heart;

And yet no man like he doth grieve my heart.

LADY CAPULET

That is, because the traitor murderer lives.

JULIET

Ay, madam, from the reach of these my hands:

Would none but I might venge my cousin's

death!

LADY CAPULET

We will have vengeance for it, fear thou not:

Then weep no more. I'll send to one in Mantua,

Where that same banish'd runagate doth live,

Shall give him such an unaccustom'd dram,

That he shall soon keep Tybalt company:

And then, I hope, thou wilt be satisfied.

JULIET

Indeed, I never shall be satisfied

With Romeo, till I behold him—dead—

Is my poor heart for a kinsman vex'd.

Madam, if you could find out but a man

To bear a poison, I would temper it;

That Romeo should, upon receipt thereof,

Soon sleep in quiet. O, how my heart abhors

To hear him named, and cannot come to him.
To wreak the love I bore my cousin
Upon his body that slaughter'd him!

LADY CAPULET

Find thou the means, and I'll find such a man.
But now I'll tell thee joyful tidings, girl.

JULIET

And joy comes well in such a needy time:
What are they, I beseech your ladyship?

LADY CAPULET

Well, well, thou hast a careful father, child;
One who, to put thee from thy heaviness,
Hath sorted out a sudden day of joy,
That thou expect'st not nor I look'd not for.

JULIET

Madam, in happy time, what day is that?

LADY CAPULET

Marry, my child, early next Thursday morn,
The gallant, young and noble gentleman,
The County Paris, at Saint Peter's Church,
Shall happily make thee there a joyful bride.

JULIET

Now, by Saint Peter's Church and Peter too,
He shall not make me there a joyful bride.
I wonder at this haste; that I must wed
Ere he, that should be husband, comes to woo.
I pray you, tell my lord and father, madam,

    I will not marry yet; and, when I do, I swear,

    It shall be Romeo, whom you know I hate,

    Rather than Paris. These are news indeed!

LADY CAPULET

    Here comes your father; tell him so yourself,

    And see how he will take it at your hands.

Enter CAPULET and Nurse

CAPULET

    When the sun sets, the air doth drizzle dew;

    But for the sunset of my brother's son

    It rains downright.

    How now! a conduit, girl? what, still in tears?

    Evermore showering? In one little body

    Thou counterfeit'st a bark, a sea, a wind;

    For still thy eyes, which I may call the sea,

    Do ebb and flow with tears; the bark thy body is,

    Sailing in this salt flood; the winds, thy sighs;

    Who, raging with thy tears, and they with them,

    Without a sudden calm, will overset

    Thy tempest-tossed body. How now, wife!

    Have you deliver'd to her our decree?

LADY CAPULET

    Ay, sir; but she will none, she gives you thanks.

    I would the fool were married to her grave!

CAPULET

    Soft! take me with you, take me with you, wife.

How! will she none? doth she not give us
    thanks?
Is she not proud? doth she not count her blest,
Unworthy as she is, that we have wrought
So worthy a gentleman to be her bridegroom?

JULIET

Not proud, you have; but thankful, that you
    have:
Proud can I never be of what I hate;
But thankful even for hate, that is meant love.

CAPULET

How now, how now, chop-logic! What is this?
'Proud,' and 'I thank you,' and 'I thank you not;'
And yet 'not proud,' mistress minion, you,
Thank me no thankings, nor, proud me no
    prouds,
But fettle your fine joints 'gainst Thursday next,
To go with Paris to Saint Peter's Church,
Or I will drag thee on a hurdle thither.
Out, you green-sickness carrion! out, you
    baggage!
You tallow-face!

LADY CAPULET

Fie, fie! what, are you mad?

JULIET

Good father, I beseech you on my knees,
Hear me with patience but to speak a word.

CAPULET

Hang thee, young baggage! disobedient wretch!

I tell thee what: get thee to church o' Thursday,

Or never after look me in the face:

Speak not, reply not, do not answer me;

My fingers itch. Wife, we scarce thought us
        blest

That God had lent us but this only child;

But now I see this one is one too much,

And that we have a curse in having her:

Out on her, hilding!

NURSE

God in heaven bless her!

You are to blame, my lord, to rate her so.

CAPULET

And why, my lady wisdom? hold your tongue,

Good prudence; smatter with your gossips, go.

NURSE

I speak no treason.

CAPULET

O, God ye god-den.

NURSE

May not one speak?

CAPULET

Peace, you mumbling fool!

Utter your gravity o'er a gossip's bowl;

For here we need it not.

LADY CAPULET

    You are too hot.

CAPULET

    God's bread! it makes me mad:
    Day, night, hour, tide, time, work, play,
    Alone, in company, still my care hath been
    To have her match'd: and having now provided
    A gentleman of noble parentage,
    Of fair demesnes, youthful, and nobly train'd,
    Stuff'd, as they say, with honourable parts,
    Proportion'd as one's thought would wish a man;
    And then to have a wretched puling fool,
    A whining mammet, in her fortune's tender,
    To answer 'I'll not wed; I cannot love,
    I am too young; I pray you, pardon me.'
    But, as you will not wed, I'll pardon you:
    Graze where you will you shall not house with
        me:
    Look to't, think on't, I do not use to jest.
    Thursday is near; lay hand on heart, advise:
    An you be mine, I'll give you to my friend;
    And you be not, hang, beg, starve, die in the
        streets,
    For, by my soul, I'll ne'er acknowledge thee,
    Nor what is mine shall never do thee good:
    Trust to't, bethink you; I'll not be forsworn.

Exit

JULIET

Is there no pity sitting in the clouds,
That sees into the bottom of my grief?
O, sweet my mother, cast me not away!
Delay this marriage for a month, a week;
Or, if you do not, make the bridal bed
In that dim monument where Tybalt lies.

LADY CAPULET

Talk not to me, for I'll not speak a word:
Do as thou wilt, for I have done with thee.

Exit

JULIET

O God!—O nurse, how shall this be prevented?
My husband is on earth, my faith in heaven;
How shall that faith return again to earth,
Unless that husband send it me from heaven
By leaving earth? comfort me, counsel me.
Alack, alack, that heaven should practise
    stratagems
Upon so soft a subject as myself!
What say'st thou? hast thou not a word of joy?
Some comfort, nurse.

NURSE

Faith, here it is.
Romeo is banish'd; and all the world to nothing,
That he dares ne'er come back to challenge you;
Or, if he do, it needs must be by stealth.

Then, since the case so stands as now it doth,
I think it best you married with the county.
O, he's a lovely gentleman!
Romeo's a dishclout to him: an eagle, madam,
Hath not so green, so quick, so fair an eye
As Paris hath. Beshrew my very heart,
I think you are happy in this second match,
For it excels your first: or if it did not,
Your first is dead; or 'twere as good he were,
As living here and you no use of him.

JULIET
Speakest thou from thy heart?

NURSE
And from my soul too;
Or else beshrew them both.

JULIET
Amen!

NURSE
What?

JULIET
Well, thou hast comforted me marvellous much.
Go in: and tell my lady I am gone,
Having displeased my father, to Laurence' cell,
To make confession and to be absolved.

NURSE
Marry, I will; and this is wisely done.

Exit

JULIET

>Ancient damnation! O most wicked fiend!
>Is it more sin to wish me thus forsworn,
>Or to dispraise my lord with that same tongue
>Which she hath praised him with above compare
>So many thousand times? Go, counsellor;
>Thou and my bosom henceforth shall be twain.
>I'll to the friar, to know his remedy:
>If all else fail, myself have power to die.

Exit

Act 4

SCENE I. FRIAR LAURENCE'S CELL.

Enter FRIAR LAURENCE and PARIS

FRIAR LAURENCE

On Thursday, sir? the time is very short.

PARIS

My father Capulet will have it so;

And I am nothing slow to slack his haste.

FRIAR LAURENCE

You say you do not know the lady's mind:

Uneven is the course, I like it not.

PARIS

Immoderately she weeps for Tybalt's death,

And therefore have I little talk'd of love;

For Venus smiles not in a house of tears.

Now, sir, her father counts it dangerous

That she doth give her sorrow so much sway,

And in his wisdom hastes our marriage,

To stop the inundation of her tears;
Which, too much minded by herself alone,
May be put from her by society:
Now do you know the reason of this haste.

FRIAR LAURENCE

(Aside) I would I knew not why it should be
slow'd.

Look, sir, here comes the lady towards my cell.

Enter JULIET

PARIS

Happily met, my lady and my wife!

JULIET

That may be, sir, when I may be a wife.

PARIS

That may be must be, love, on Thursday next.

JULIET

What must be shall be.

FRIAR LAURENCE

That's a certain text.

PARIS

Come you to make confession to this father?

JULIET

To answer that, I should confess to you.

PARIS

Do not deny to him that you love me.

JULIET

I will confess to you that I love him.

PARIS

So will ye, I am sure, that you love me.

JULIET

If I do so, it will be of more price,

Being spoke behind your back, than to your face.

PARIS

Poor soul, thy face is much abused with tears.

JULIET

The tears have got small victory by that;

For it was bad enough before their spite.

PARIS

Thou wrong'st it, more than tears, with that report.

JULIET

That is no slander, sir, which is a truth;

And what I spake, I spake it to my face.

PARIS

Thy face is mine, and thou hast slander'd it.

JULIET

It may be so, for it is not mine own.

Are you at leisure, holy father, now;

Or shall I come to you at evening mass?

FRIAR LAURENCE

My leisure serves me, pensive daughter, now.

My lord, we must entreat the time alone.

PARIS

God shield I should disturb devotion!
Juliet, on Thursday early will I rouse ye:
Till then, adieu; and keep this holy kiss.

Exit

JULIET

O shut the door! and when thou hast done so,
Come weep with me; past hope, past cure, past
   help!

FRIAR LAURENCE

Ah, Juliet, I already know thy grief;
It strains me past the compass of my wits:
I hear thou must, and nothing may prorogue it,
On Thursday next be married to this county.

JULIET

Tell me not, friar, that thou hear'st of this,
Unless thou tell me how I may prevent it:
If, in thy wisdom, thou canst give no help,
Do thou but call my resolution wise,
And with this knife I'll help it presently.
God join'd my heart and Romeo's, thou our
   hands;
And ere this hand, by thee to Romeo seal'd,
Shall be the label to another deed,
Or my true heart with treacherous revolt
Turn to another, this shall slay them both:
Therefore, out of thy long-experienced time,
Give me some present counsel, or, behold,

'Twixt my extremes and me this bloody knife
Shall play the umpire, arbitrating that
Which the commission of thy years and art
Could to no issue of true honour bring.
Be not so long to speak; I long to die,
If what thou speak'st speak not of remedy.

FRIAR LAURENCE

Hold, daughter: I do spy a kind of hope,
Which craves as desperate an execution.
As that is desperate which we would prevent.
If, rather than to marry County Paris,
Thou hast the strength of will to slay thyself,
Then is it likely thou wilt undertake
A thing like death to chide away this shame,
That copest with death himself to scape from it:
And, if thou darest, I'll give thee remedy.

JULIET

O, bid me leap, rather than marry Paris,
From off the battlements of yonder tower;
Or walk in thievish ways; or bid me lurk
Where serpents are; chain me with roaring
    bears;
Or shut me nightly in a charnel-house,
O'er-cover'd quite with dead men's rattling
    bones,
With reeky shanks and yellow chapless skulls;
Or bid me go into a new-made grave

And hide me with a dead man in his shroud;
Things that, to hear them told, have made me
    tremble;
And I will do it without fear or doubt,
To live an unstain'd wife to my sweet love.

FRIAR LAURENCE

Hold, then; go home, be merry, give consent
To marry Paris: Wednesday is to-morrow:
To-morrow night look that thou lie alone;
Let not thy nurse lie with thee in thy chamber:
Take thou this vial, being then in bed,
And this distilled liquor drink thou off;
When presently through all thy veins shall run
A cold and drowsy humour, for no pulse
Shall keep his native progress, but surcease:
No warmth, no breath, shall testify thou livest;
The roses in thy lips and cheeks shall fade
To paly ashes, thy eyes' windows fall,
Like death, when he shuts up the day of life;
Each part, deprived of supple government,
Shall, stiff and stark and cold, appear like death:
And in this borrow'd likeness of shrunk death
Thou shalt continue two and forty hours,
And then awake as from a pleasant sleep.
Now, when the bridegroom in the morning
    comes
To rouse thee from thy bed, there art thou

dead:
Then, as the manner of our country is,
In thy best robes uncover'd on the bier
Thou shalt be borne to that same ancient vault
Where all the kindred of the Capulets lie.
In the mean time, against thou shalt awake,
Shall Romeo by my letters know our drift,
And hither shall he come: and he and I
Will watch thy waking, and that very night
Shall Romeo bear thee hence to Mantua.
And this shall free thee from this present shame;
If no inconstant toy, nor womanish fear,
Abate thy valour in the acting it.

JULIET
Give me, give me! O, tell not me of fear!

FRIAR LAURENCE
Hold; get you gone, be strong and prosperous
In this resolve: I'll send a friar with speed
To Mantua, with my letters to thy lord.

JULIET
Love give me strength! and strength shall help
afford.
Farewell, dear father!

Exeunt.

SCENE II. HALL IN CAPULET'S HOUSE.

Enter CAPULET, LADY CAPULET, Nurse, and two Servingmen

CAPULET

So many guests invite as here are writ.

Exit First Servant

Sirrah, go hire me twenty cunning cooks.

SECOND SERVANT

You shall have none ill, sir; for I'll try if they can lick their fingers.

CAPULET

How canst thou try them so?

SECOND SERVANT

Marry, sir, 'tis an ill cook that cannot lick his own fingers: therefore he that cannot lick his fingers goes not with me.

CAPULET

Go, be gone.

Exit Second Servant

We shall be much unfurnished for this time.
What, is my daughter gone to Friar Laurence?

NURSE

Ay, forsooth.

CAPULET

Well, he may chance to do some good on her:
A peevish self-will'd harlotry it is.

NURSE

> See where she comes from shrift with merry
> look.

Enter JULIET

CAPULET

> How now, my headstrong! where have you
> been gadding?

JULIET

> Where I have learn'd me to repent the sin
> Of disobedient opposition
> To you and your behests, and am enjoin'd
> By holy Laurence to fall prostrate here,
> And beg your pardon: pardon, I beseech you!
> Henceforward I am ever ruled by you.

CAPULET

> Send for the county; go tell him of this:
> I'll have this knot knit up to-morrow morning.

JULIET

> I met the youthful lord at Laurence' cell;
> And gave him what becomed love I might,
> Not step o'er the bounds of modesty.

CAPULET

> Why, I am glad on't; this is well: stand up:
> This is as't should be. Let me see the county;
> Ay, marry, go, I say, and fetch him hither.

Now, afore God! this reverend holy friar,
Our whole city is much bound to him.

JULIET

Nurse, will you go with me into my closet,
To help me sort such needful ornaments
As you think fit to furnish me to-morrow?

LADY CAPULET

No, not till Thursday; there is time enough.

CAPULET

Go, nurse, go with her: we'll to church to-
morrow.

Exeunt JULIET and Nurse

LADY CAPULET

We shall be short in our provision:
'Tis now near night.

CAPULET

Tush, I will stir about,
And all things shall be well, I warrant thee, wife:
Go thou to Juliet, help to deck up her;
I'll not to bed to-night; let me alone;
I'll play the housewife for this once. What, ho!
They are all forth. Well, I will walk myself
To County Paris, to prepare him up
Against to-morrow: my heart is wondrous light,
Since this same wayward girl is so reclaim'd.

Exeunt

SCENE III. JULIET'S CHAMBER.

Enter JULIET and Nurse

JULIET

    Ay, those attires are best: but, gentle nurse,

    I pray thee, leave me to my self to-night,

    For I have need of many orisons

    To move the heavens to smile upon my state,

    Which, well thou know'st, is cross, and full of

        sin.

Enter LADY CAPULET

LADY CAPULET

    What, are you busy, ho? need you my help?

JULIET

    No, madam; we have cull'd such necessaries

    As are behoveful for our state to-morrow:

    So please you, let me now be left alone,

    And let the nurse this night sit up with you;

    For, I am sure, you have your hands full all,

    In this so sudden business.

LADY CAPULET

    Good night:

    Get thee to bed, and rest; for thou hast need.

                    Exeunt LADY CAPULET and Nurse

JULIET

> Farewell! God knows when we shall meet
> again.
> I have a faint cold fear thrills through my veins,
> That almost freezes up the heat of life:
> I'll call them back again to comfort me:
> Nurse! What should she do here?
> My dismal scene I needs must act alone.
> Come, vial.
> What if this mixture do not work at all?
> Shall I be married then to-morrow morning?
> No, no: this shall forbid it: lie thou there.

Laying down her dagger

> What if it be a poison, which the friar
> Subtly hath minister'd to have me dead,
> Lest in this marriage he should be dishonour'd,
> Because he married me before to Romeo?
> I fear it is: and yet, methinks, it should not,
> For he hath still been tried a holy man.
> How if, when I am laid into the tomb,
> I wake before the time that Romeo
> Come to redeem me? there's a fearful point!
> Shall I not, then, be stifled in the vault,
> To whose foul mouth no healthsome air
> breathes in,
> And there die strangled ere my Romeo comes?
> Or, if I live, is it not very like,

The horrible conceit of death and night,
Together with the terror of the place,—
As in a vault, an ancient receptacle,
Where, for these many hundred years, the
    bones
Of all my buried ancestors are packed:
Where bloody Tybalt, yet but green in earth,
Lies festering in his shroud; where, as they say,
At some hours in the night spirits resort;—
Alack, alack, is it not like that I,
So early waking, what with loathsome smells,
And shrieks like mandrakes' torn out of the
    earth,
That living mortals, hearing them, run mad:—
O, if I wake, shall I not be distraught,
Environed with all these hideous fears?
And madly play with my forefather's joints?
And pluck the mangled Tybalt from his
    shroud?
And, in this rage, with some great kinsman's
    bone,
As with a club, dash out my desperate brains?
O, look! methinks I see my cousin's ghost
Seeking out Romeo, that did spit his body
Upon a rapier's point: stay, Tybalt, stay!
Romeo, I come! this do I drink to thee.
She falls upon her bed, within the curtains

SCENE IV. HALL IN CAPULET'S HOUSE.

Enter LADY CAPULET and Nurse

LADY CAPULET

> Hold, take these keys, and fetch more spices, nurse.

NURSE

> They call for dates and quinces in the pastry.

Enter CAPULET

CAPULET

> Come, stir, stir, stir! the second cock hath crow'd,
> The curfew-bell hath rung, 'tis three o'clock:
> Look to the baked meats, good Angelica:
> Spare not for the cost.

NURSE

> Go, you cot-quean, go,
> Get you to bed; faith, You'll be sick to-morrow
> For this night's watching.

CAPULET

> No, not a whit: what! I have watch'd ere now
> All night for lesser cause, and ne'er been sick.

LADY CAPULET

> Ay, you have been a mouse-hunt in your time;
> But I will watch you from such watching now.
>
> *Exeunt LADY CAPULET and Nurse*

CAPULET

A jealous hood, a jealous hood!

Enter three or four Servingmen, with spits, logs, and baskets

Now, fellow,

What's there?

FIRST SERVANT

Things for the cook, sir; but I know not what.

CAPULET

Make haste, make haste.

Exit First Servant

Sirrah, fetch drier logs:

Call Peter, he will show thee where they are.

SECOND SERVANT

I have a head, sir, that will find out logs,

And never trouble Peter for the matter.

Exit

CAPULET

Mass, and well said; a merry whoreson, ha!

Thou shalt be logger-head. Good faith, 'tis
day:

The county will be here with music straight,

For so he said he would: I hear him near.

Music within

Nurse! Wife! What, ho! What, nurse, I say!

Re-enter Nurse

Go waken Juliet, go and trim her up;

I'll go and chat with Paris: hie, make haste,
Make haste; the bridegroom he is come already:
Make haste, I say.

Exeunt

SCENE V. JULIET'S CHAMBER.

Enter NURSE
NURSE

Mistress! what, mistress! Juliet! fast, I warrant
    her, she:
Why, lamb! why, lady! fie, you slug-a-bed!
Why, love, I say! madam! sweet-heart! why,
    bride!
What, not a word? you take your pennyworths
    now;
Sleep for a week; for the next night, I warrant,
The County Paris hath set up his rest,
That you shall rest but little. God forgive me,
Marry, and amen, how sound is she asleep!
I must needs wake her. Madam, madam,
    madam!
Ay, let the county take you in your bed;
He'll fright you up, i' faith. Will it not be?
Undraws the curtains
What, dress'd! and in your clothes! and down
    again!

I must needs wake you; Lady! lady! lady!
Alas, alas! Help, help! my lady's dead!
O, well-a-day, that ever I was born!
Some aqua vitae, ho! My lord! my lady!

Enter LADY CAPULET
LADY CAPULET
What noise is here?
NURSE
O lamentable day!
LADY CAPULET
What is the matter?
NURSE
Look, look! O heavy day!
LADY CAPULET
O me, O me! My child, my only life,
Revive, look up, or I will die with thee!
Help, help! Call help.

Enter CAPULET
CAPULET
For shame, bring Juliet forth; her lord is come.
NURSE
She's dead, deceased, she's dead; alack the day!
LADY CAPULET
Alack the day, she's dead, she's dead, she's
dead!

CAPULET

Ha! let me see her: out, alas! she's cold:

Her blood is settled, and her joints are stiff;

Life and these lips have long been separated:

Death lies on her like an untimely frost

Upon the sweetest flower of all the field.

NURSE

O lamentable day!

LADY CAPULET

O woful time!

CAPULET

Death, that hath ta'en her hence to make me
wail,

Ties up my tongue, and will not let me speak.

*Enter FRIAR LAURENCE and PARIS, with
Musicians*

FRIAR LAURENCE

Come, is the bride ready to go to church?

CAPULET

Ready to go, but never to return.

O son! the night before thy wedding-day

Hath Death lain with thy wife. There she lies,

Flower as she was, deflowered by him.

Death is my son-in-law, Death is my heir;

My daughter he hath wedded: I will die,

And leave him all; life, living, all is Death's.

PARIS

Have I thought long to see this morning's face,
And doth it give me such a sight as this?

LADY CAPULET

Accursed, unhappy, wretched, hateful day!
Most miserable hour that e'er time saw
In lasting labour of his pilgrimage!
But one, poor one, one poor and loving child,
But one thing to rejoice and solace in,
And cruel death hath catch'd it from my sight!

NURSE

O woe! O woful, woful, woful day!
Most lamentable day, most woful day,
That ever, ever, I did yet behold!
O day! O day! O day! O hateful day!
Never was seen so black a day as this:
O woful day, O woful day!

PARIS

Beguiled, divorced, wronged, spited, slain!
Most detestable death, by thee beguil'd,
By cruel cruel thee quite overthrown!
O love! O life! not life, but love in death!

CAPULET

Despised, distressed, hated, martyr'd, kill'd!
Uncomfortable time, why camest thou now
To murder, murder our solemnity?
O child! O child! my soul, and not my child!

Dead art thou! Alack! my child is dead;
And with my child my joys are buried.
FRIAR LAURENCE
Peace, ho, for shame! confusion's cure lives not
In these confusions. Heaven and yourself
Had part in this fair maid; now heaven hath
all,
And all the better is it for the maid:
Your part in her you could not keep from
death,
But heaven keeps his part in eternal life.
The most you sought was her promotion;
For 'twas your heaven she should be advanced:
And weep ye now, seeing she is advanced
Above the clouds, as high as heaven itself?
O, in this love, you love your child so ill,
That you run mad, seeing that she is well:
She's not well married that lives married long;
But she's best married that dies married young.
Dry up your tears, and stick your rosemary
On this fair corse; and, as the custom is,
In all her best array bear her to church:
For though fond nature bids us an lament,
Yet nature's tears are reason's merriment.
CAPULET
All things that we ordained festival,
Turn from their office to black funeral;

Our instruments to melancholy bells,
Our wedding cheer to a sad burial feast,
Our solemn hymns to sullen dirges change,
Our bridal flowers serve for a buried corse,
And all things change them to the contrary.

FRIAR LAURENCE

Sir, go you in; and, madam, go with him;
And go, Sir Paris; every one prepare
To follow this fair corse unto her grave:
The heavens do lour upon you for some ill;
Move them no more by crossing their high will.

Exeunt CAPULET, LADY CAPULET,
PARIS, and FRIAR LAURENCE

FIRST MUSICIAN

Faith, we may put up our pipes, and be gone.

NURSE

Honest goodfellows, ah, put up, put up;
For, well you know, this is a pitiful case.

Exit

FIRST MUSICIAN

Ay, by my troth, the case may be amended.

Enter PETER

PETER

Musicians, O, musicians, 'Heart's ease, Heart's
ease:' O, an you will have me live, play 'Heart's
ease.'

FIRST MUSICIAN

Why 'Heart's ease?'

PETER

O, musicians, because my heart itself plays 'My heart is full of woe:' O, play me some merry dump, to comfort me.

FIRST MUSICIAN

Not a dump we; 'tis no time to play now.

PETER

You will not, then?

FIRST MUSICIAN

No.

PETER

I will then give it you soundly.

FIRST MUSICIAN

What will you give us?

PETER

No money, on my faith, but the gleek;
I will give you the minstrel.

FIRST MUSICIAN

Then I will give you the serving-creature.

PETER

Then will I lay the serving-creature's dagger on your pate. I will carry no crotchets: I'll re you, I'll fa you; do you note me?

FIRST MUSICIAN

An you re us and fa us, you note us.

SECOND MUSICIAN

Pray you, put up your dagger, and put out your wit.

PETER

Then have at you with my wit! I will dry-beat you with an iron wit, and put up my iron dagger.

Answer me like men:

'When griping grief the heart doth wound,
And doleful dumps the mind oppress,
Then music with her silver sound'—

why 'silver sound'? why 'music with her silver sound'? What say you, Simon Catling?

MUSICIAN

Marry, sir, because silver hath a sweet sound.

PETER

Pretty! What say you, Hugh Rebeck?

SECOND MUSICIAN

I say 'silver sound,' because musicians sound for silver.

PETER

Pretty too! What say you, James Soundpost?

THIRD MUSICIAN

Faith, I know not what to say.

PETER

O, I cry you mercy; you are the singer: I will say for you. It is 'music with her silver sound,'

because musicians have no gold for sounding:
'Then music with her silver sound With speedy
help doth lend redress.'

Exit

FIRST MUSICIAN

What a pestilent knave is this same!

SECOND MUSICIAN

Hang him, Jack! Come, we'll in here; tarry for
the mourners, and stay dinner.

Exeunt

Act 5

SCENE I. MANTUA. A STREET.

Enter ROMEO

ROMEO

    If I may trust the flattering truth of sleep,
    My dreams presage some joyful news at hand:
    My bosom's lord sits lightly in his throne;
    And all this day an unaccustom'd spirit
    Lifts me above the ground with cheerful
        thoughts.
    I dreamt my lady came and found me dead—
    Strange dream, that gives a dead man leave to
        think!—
    And breathed such life with kisses in my lips,
    That I revived, and was an emperor.
    Ah me! how sweet is love itself possess'd,
    When but love's shadows are so rich in joy!

Enter BALTHASAR, booted

News from Verona!—How now, Balthasar!
Dost thou not bring me letters from the friar?
How doth my lady? Is my father well?
How fares my Juliet? that I ask again;
For nothing can be ill, if she be well.

BALTHASAR

Then she is well, and nothing can be ill:
Her body sleeps in Capel's monument,
And her immortal part with angels lives.
I saw her laid low in her kindred's vault,
And presently took post to tell it you:
O, pardon me for bringing these ill news,
Since you did leave it for my office, sir.

ROMEO

Is it even so? then I defy you, stars!
Thou know'st my lodging: get me ink and
    paper,
And hire post-horses; I will hence to-night.

BALTHASAR

I do beseech you, sir, have patience:
Your looks are pale and wild, and do import
Some misadventure.

ROMEO

Tush, thou art deceived:
Leave me, and do the thing I bid thee do.
Hast thou no letters to me from the friar?

BALTHASAR

No, my good lord.

ROMEO

No matter: get thee gone,
And hire those horses; I'll be with thee straight.

Exit BALTHASAR

Well, Juliet, I will lie with thee to-night.
Let's see for means: O mischief, thou art swift
To enter in the thoughts of desperate men!
I do remember an apothecary,—
And hereabouts he dwells,—which late I noted
In tatter'd weeds, with overwhelming brows,
Culling of simples; meagre were his looks,
Sharp misery had worn him to the bones:
And in his needy shop a tortoise hung,
An alligator stuff'd, and other skins
Of ill-shaped fishes; and about his shelves
A beggarly account of empty boxes,
Green earthen pots, bladders and musty seeds,
Remnants of packthread and old cakes of
    roses,
Were thinly scatter'd, to make up a show.
Noting this penury, to myself I said
'An if a man did need a poison now,
Whose sale is present death in Mantua,
Here lives a caitiff wretch would sell it him.'
O, this same thought did but forerun my need;

And this same needy man must sell it me.
As I remember, this should be the house.
Being holiday, the beggar's shop is shut.
What, ho! apothecary!

Enter Apothecary
APOTHECARY

Who calls so loud?
ROMEO

Come hither, man. I see that thou art poor:
Hold, there is forty ducats: let me have
A dram of poison, such soon-speeding gear
As will disperse itself through all the veins
That the life-weary taker may fall dead
And that the trunk may be discharged of
     breath
As violently as hasty powder fired
Doth hurry from the fatal cannon's womb.
APOTHECARY

Such mortal drugs I have; but Mantua's law
Is death to any he that utters them.
ROMEO

Art thou so bare and full of wretchedness,
And fear'st to die? famine is in thy cheeks,
Need and oppression starveth in thine eyes,
Contempt and beggary hangs upon thy back;
The world is not thy friend nor the world's law;

The world affords no law to make thee rich;
Then be not poor, but break it, and take this.

APOTHECARY

My poverty, but not my will, consents.

ROMEO

I pay thy poverty, and not thy will.

APOTHECARY

Put this in any liquid thing you will,
And drink it off; and, if you had the strength
Of twenty men, it would dispatch you straight.

ROMEO

There is thy gold, worse poison to men's souls,
Doing more murders in this loathsome world,
Than these poor compounds that thou mayst
    not sell.
I sell thee poison; thou hast sold me none.
Farewell: buy food, and get thyself in flesh.
Come, cordial and not poison, go with me
To Juliet's grave; for there must I use thee.

Exeunt

SCENE II. FRIAR LAURENCE'S CELL.

Enter FRIAR JOHN
FRIAR JOHN

    Holy Franciscan friar! brother, ho!

Enter FRIAR LAURENCE
FRIAR LAURENCE

    This same should be the voice of Friar John.
    Welcome from Mantua: what says Romeo?
    Or, if his mind be writ, give me his letter.

FRIAR JOHN

    Going to find a bare-foot brother out
    One of our order, to associate me,
    Here in this city visiting the sick,
    And finding him, the searchers of the town,
    Suspecting that we both were in a house
    Where the infectious pestilence did reign,
    Seal'd up the doors, and would not let us forth;
    So that my speed to Mantua there was stay'd.

FRIAR LAURENCE

    Who bare my letter, then, to Romeo?

FRIAR JOHN

    I could not send it,—here it is again,—
    Nor get a messenger to bring it thee,
    So fearful were they of infection.

FRIAR LAURENCE

Unhappy fortune! by my brotherhood,
The letter was not nice but full of charge
Of dear import, and the neglecting it
May do much danger. Friar John, go hence;
Get me an iron crow, and bring it straight
Unto my cell.

FRIAR JOHN

Brother, I'll go and bring it thee.

Exit

FRIAR LAURENCE

Now must I to the monument alone;
Within three hours will fair Juliet wake:
She will beshrew me much that Romeo
Hath had no notice of these accidents;
But I will write again to Mantua,
And keep her at my cell till Romeo come;
Poor living corse, closed in a dead man's tomb!

Exit

SCENE III. A CHURCHYARD; IN IT A TOMB BELONGING TO THE CAPULETS.

Enter PARIS, and his Page bearing flowers and a torch
PARIS

> Give me thy torch, boy: hence, and stand aloof:
> Yet put it out, for I would not be seen.
> Under yond yew-trees lay thee all along,
> Holding thine ear close to the hollow ground;
> So shall no foot upon the churchyard tread,
> Being loose, unfirm, with digging up of graves,
> But thou shalt hear it: whistle then to me,
> As signal that thou hear'st something approach.
> Give me those flowers. Do as I bid thee, go.

PAGE (ASIDE)

> I am almost afraid to stand alone
> Here in the churchyard; yet I will adventure.
> *Retires*

PARIS

> Sweet flower, with flowers thy bridal bed I
> strew,—
> O woe! thy canopy is dust and stones;—
> Which with sweet water nightly I will dew,
> Or, wanting that, with tears distill'd by moans:
> The obsequies that I for thee will keep
> Nightly shall be to strew thy grave and weep.
> *The Page whistles*

The boy gives warning something doth
    approach.
What cursed foot wanders this way to-night,
To cross my obsequies and true love's rite?
What with a torch! muffle me, night, awhile.
Retires

*Enter ROMEO and BALTHASAR, with a torch,
mattock, & c*
ROMEO
    Give me that mattock and the wrenching iron.
    Hold, take this letter; early in the morning
    See thou deliver it to my lord and father.
    Give me the light: upon thy life, I charge thee,
    Whate'er thou hear'st or seest, stand all aloof,
    And do not interrupt me in my course.
    Why I descend into this bed of death,
    Is partly to behold my lady's face;
    But chiefly to take thence from her dead finger
    A precious ring, a ring that I must use
    In dear employment: therefore hence, be gone:
    But if thou, jealous, dost return to pry
    In what I further shall intend to do,
    By heaven, I will tear thee joint by joint
    And strew this hungry churchyard with thy
        limbs:
    The time and my intents are savage-wild,

More fierce and more inexorable far
Than empty tigers or the roaring sea.

BALTHASAR

I will be gone, sir, and not trouble you.

ROMEO

So shalt thou show me friendship. Take thou
that:

Live, and be prosperous: and farewell, good
fellow.

BALTHASAR

(Aside) For all this same, I'll hide me hereabout:
His looks I fear, and his intents I doubt.
Retires

ROMEO

Thou detestable maw, thou womb of death,
Gorged with the dearest morsel of the earth,
Thus I enforce thy rotten jaws to open,
And, in despite, I'll cram thee with more food!
Opens the tomb

PARIS

This is that banish'd haughty Montague,
That murder'd my love's cousin, with which
grief,
It is supposed, the fair creature died;
And here is come to do some villanous shame
To the dead bodies: I will apprehend him.
Comes forward

Stop thy unhallow'd toil, vile Montague!
Can vengeance be pursued further than death?
Condemned villain, I do apprehend thee:
Obey, and go with me; for thou must die.

ROMEO

I must indeed; and therefore came I hither.
Good gentle youth, tempt not a desperate man;
Fly hence, and leave me: think upon these gone;
Let them affright thee. I beseech thee, youth,
Put not another sin upon my head,
By urging me to fury: O, be gone!
By heaven, I love thee better than myself;
For I come hither arm'd against myself:
Stay not, be gone; live, and hereafter say,
A madman's mercy bade thee run away.

PARIS

I do defy thy conjurations,
And apprehend thee for a felon here.

ROMEO

Wilt thou provoke me? then have at thee, boy!

They fight

PAGE

O Lord, they fight! I will go call the watch.

Exit

PARIS

O, I am slain!

Falls

If thou be merciful,
Open the tomb, lay me with Juliet.

Dies

ROMEO

In faith, I will. Let me peruse this face.
Mercutio's kinsman, noble County Paris!
What said my man, when my betossed soul
Did not attend him as we rode? I think
He told me Paris should have married Juliet:
Said he not so? or did I dream it so?
Or am I mad, hearing him talk of Juliet,
To think it was so? O, give me thy hand,
One writ with me in sour misfortune's book!
I'll bury thee in a triumphant grave;
A grave? O no! a lantern, slaughter'd youth,
For here lies Juliet, and her beauty makes
This vault a feasting presence full of light.
Death, lie thou there, by a dead man interr'd.

Laying PARIS in the tomb

How oft when men are at the point of death
Have they been merry! which their keepers call
A lightning before death: O, how may I
Call this a lightning? O my love! my wife!
Death, that hath suck'd the honey of thy breath,
Hath had no power yet upon thy beauty:
Thou art not conquer'd; beauty's ensign yet
Is crimson in thy lips and in thy cheeks,

And death's pale flag is not advanced there.
Tybalt, liest thou there in thy bloody sheet?
O, what more favour can I do to thee,
Than with that hand that cut thy youth in twain
To sunder his that was thine enemy?
Forgive me, cousin! Ah, dear Juliet,
Why art thou yet so fair? shall I believe
That unsubstantial death is amorous,
And that the lean abhorred monster keeps
Thee here in dark to be his paramour?
For fear of that, I still will stay with thee;
And never from this palace of dim night
Depart again: here, here will I remain
With worms that are thy chamber-maids; O,
      here
Will I set up my everlasting rest,
And shake the yoke of inauspicious stars
From this world-wearied flesh. Eyes, look your
      last!
Arms, take your last embrace! and, lips, O you
The doors of breath, seal with a righteous kiss
A dateless bargain to engrossing death!
Come, bitter conduct, come, unsavoury guide!
Thou desperate pilot, now at once run on
The dashing rocks thy sea-sick weary bark!
Here's to my love!
Drinks

O true apothecary!
Thy drugs are quick. Thus with a kiss I die.
Dies

*Enter, at the other end of the churchyard, FRIAR
LAURENCE, with a lantern, crow, and spade*
FRIAR LAURENCE

Saint Francis be my speed! how oft to-night
Have my old feet stumbled at graves! Who's
   there?
BALTHASAR

Here's one, a friend, and one that knows you
well.
FRIAR LAURENCE

Bliss be upon you! Tell me, good my friend,
What torch is yond, that vainly lends his light
To grubs and eyeless skulls? as I discern,
It burneth in the Capel's monument.
BALTHASAR

It doth so, holy sir; and there's my master,
One that you love.
FRIAR LAURENCE

Who is it?
BALTHASAR

Romeo.
FRIAR LAURENCE

How long hath he been there?

BALTHASAR

Full half an hour.

FRIAR LAURENCE

Go with me to the vault.

BALTHASAR

I dare not, sir

My master knows not but I am gone hence;

And fearfully did menace me with death,

If I did stay to look on his intents.

FRIAR LAURENCE

Stay, then; I'll go alone. Fear comes upon me:

O, much I fear some ill unlucky thing.

BALTHASAR

As I did sleep under this yew-tree here,

I dreamt my master and another fought,

And that my master slew him.

FRIAR LAURENCE

Romeo!

Advances

Alack, alack, what blood is this, which stains

The stony entrance of this sepulchre?

What mean these masterless and gory swords

To lie discolour'd by this place of peace?

Enters the tomb

Romeo! O, pale! Who else? what, Paris too?

And steep'd in blood? Ah, what an unkind hour

Is guilty of this lamentable chance!
The lady stirs.
JULIET wakes

JULIET

O comfortable friar! where is my lord?
I do remember well where I should be,
And there I am. Where is my Romeo?
Noise within

FRIAR LAURENCE

I hear some noise. Lady, come from that nest
Of death, contagion, and unnatural sleep:
A greater power than we can contradict
Hath thwarted our intents. Come, come away.
Thy husband in thy bosom there lies dead;
And Paris too. Come, I'll dispose of thee
Among a sisterhood of holy nuns:
Stay not to question, for the watch is coming;
Come, go, good Juliet,
Noise again
I dare no longer stay.

JULIET

Go, get thee hence, for I will not away.
Exit FRIAR LAURENCE
What's here? a cup, closed in my true love's hand?
Poison, I see, hath been his timeless end:
O churl! drunk all, and left no friendly drop
To help me after? I will kiss thy lips;

Haply some poison yet doth hang on them,
To make die with a restorative.

Kisses him

Thy lips are warm.

FIRST WATCHMAN

(Within) Lead, boy: which way?

JULIET

Yea, noise? then I'll be brief. O happy dagger!

Snatching ROMEO's dagger

This is thy sheath;

Stabs herself

there rust, and let me die.

Falls on ROMEO's body, and dies

Enter Watch, with the Page of PARIS

PAGE

This is the place; there, where the torch doth
burn.

FIRST WATCHMAN

The ground is bloody; search about the
churchyard:

Go, some of you, whoe'er you find attach.

Pitiful sight! here lies the county slain,

And Juliet bleeding, warm, and newly dead,

Who here hath lain these two days buried.

Go, tell the prince: run to the Capulets:

Raise up the Montagues: some others search:

We see the ground whereon these woes do lie;
But the true ground of all these piteous woes
We cannot without circumstance descry.

Re-enter some of the Watch, with BALTHASAR
SECOND WATCHMAN
Here's Romeo's man; we found him in the
churchyard.
FIRST WATCHMAN
Hold him in safety, till the prince come hither.

Re-enter others of the Watch, with FRIAR LAURENCE
THIRD WATCHMAN
Here is a friar, that trembles, sighs and weeps:
We took this mattock and this spade from him,
As he was coming from this churchyard side.
FIRST WATCHMAN
A great suspicion: stay the friar too.

Enter the PRINCE *and Attendants*
PRINCE
What misadventure is so early up,
That calls our person from our morning's rest?

Enter CAPULET, LADY CAPULET, *and others*
CAPULET
What should it be, that they so shriek abroad?

LADY CAPULET

> The people in the street cry Romeo,
> Some Juliet, and some Paris; and all run,
> With open outcry toward our monument.

PRINCE

> What fear is this which startles in our ears?

FIRST WATCHMAN

> Sovereign, here lies the County Paris slain;
> And Romeo dead; and Juliet, dead before,
> Warm and new kill'd.

PRINCE

> Search, seek, and know how this foul murder
> comes.

FIRST WATCHMAN

> Here is a friar, and slaughter'd Romeo's man;
> With instruments upon them, fit to open
> These dead men's tombs.

CAPULET

> O heavens! O wife, look how our daughter
> bleeds!
> This dagger hath mista'en—for, lo, his house
> Is empty on the back of Montague,—
> And it mis-sheathed in my daughter's bosom!

LADY CAPULET

> O me! this sight of death is as a bell,
> That warns my old age to a sepulchre.

Enter MONTAGUE and others

PRINCE

Come, Montague; for thou art early up,

To see thy son and heir more early down.

MONTAGUE

Alas, my liege, my wife is dead to-night;

Grief of my son's exile hath stopp'd her
    breath:

What further woe conspires against mine age?

PRINCE

Look, and thou shalt see.

MONTAGUE

O thou untaught! what manners is in this? To

press before thy father to a grave?

PRINCE

Seal up the mouth of outrage for a while,

Till we can clear these ambiguities,

And know their spring, their head, their true
    descent;

And then will I be general of your woes,

And lead you even to death: meantime forbear,

And let mischance be slave to patience.

Bring forth the parties of suspicion.

FRIAR LAURENCE

I am the greatest, able to do least,

Yet most suspected, as the time and place

Doth make against me of this direful murder;

And here I stand, both to impeach and purge
Myself condemned and myself excused.

PRINCE

Then say at once what thou dost know in this.

FRIAR LAURENCE

I will be brief, for my short date of breath
Is not so long as is a tedious tale.
Romeo, there dead, was husband to that Juliet;
And she, there dead, that Romeo's faithful wife:
I married them; and their stol'n marriage-day
Was Tybalt's dooms-day, whose untimely death
Banish'd the new-made bridegroom from the
    city,
For whom, and not for Tybalt, Juliet pined.
You, to remove that siege of grief from her,
Betroth'd and would have married her perforce
To County Paris: then comes she to me,
And, with wild looks, bid me devise some mean
To rid her from this second marriage,
Or in my cell there would she kill herself.
Then gave I her, so tutor'd by my art,
A sleeping potion; which so took effect
As I intended, for it wrought on her
The form of death: meantime I writ to Romeo,
That he should hither come as this dire night,
To help to take her from her borrow'd grave,
Being the time the potion's force should cease.

But he which bore my letter, Friar John,
Was stay'd by accident, and yesternight
Return'd my letter back. Then all alone
At the prefixed hour of her waking,
Came I to take her from her kindred's vault;
Meaning to keep her closely at my cell,
Till I conveniently could send to Romeo:
But when I came, some minute ere the time
Of her awaking, here untimely lay
The noble Paris and true Romeo dead.
She wakes; and I entreated her come forth,
And bear this work of heaven with patience:
But then a noise did scare me from the tomb;
And she, too desperate, would not go with me,
But, as it seems, did violence on herself.
All this I know; and to the marriage
Her nurse is privy: and, if aught in this
Miscarried by my fault, let my old life
Be sacrificed, some hour before his time,
Unto the rigour of severest law.

PRINCE

We still have known thee for a holy man.
Where's Romeo's man? what can he say in this?

BALTHASAR

I brought my master news of Juliet's death;
And then in post he came from Mantua
To this same place, to this same monument.

    This letter he early bid me give his father,
    And threatened me with death, going in the
        vault,
    I departed not and left him there.

PRINCE

    Give me the letter; I will look on it.
    Where is the county's page, that raised the
        watch?
    Sirrah, what made your master in this place?

PAGE

    He came with flowers to strew his lady's grave;
    And bid me stand aloof, and so I did:
    Anon comes one with light to ope the tomb;
    And by and by my master drew on him;
    And then I ran away to call the watch.

PRINCE

    This letter doth make good the friar's words,
    Their course of love, the tidings of her death:
    And here he writes that he did buy a poison
    Of a poor 'pothecary, and therewithal
    Came to this vault to die, and lie with Juliet.
    Where be these enemies? Capulet! Montague!
    See, what a scourge is laid upon your hate,
    That heaven finds means to kill your joys with
        love.
    And I for winking at your discords too
    Have lost a brace of kinsmen: all are punish'd.

CAPULET

> O brother Montague, give me thy hand:
> This is my daughter's jointure, for no more
> Can I demand.

MONTAGUE

> But I can give thee more:
> For I will raise her statue in pure gold;
> That while Verona by that name is known,
> There shall no figure at such rate be set
> As that of true and faithful Juliet.

CAPULET

> As rich shall Romeo's by his lady's lie;
> Poor sacrifices of our enmity!

PRINCE

> A glooming peace this morning with it brings;
> The sun, for sorrow, will not show his head:
> Go hence, to have more talk of these sad
>   things;
> Some shall be pardon'd, and some punished:
> For never was a story of more woe
> Than this of Juliet and her Romeo.

Exeunt